Listen Like A Horse

Relationships Without Dominance

How To Help Your Horse Feel Safe With You

"This feels like it goes much deeper than horses."

For more assistance and one aproach to applying your own innate ability to communicate, you can purchase a DVD on the website, or watch online.

http://www.kerrilake.com/products.html, or watch at
http://www.youtube.com/watch?v=h-A1f1r5OJU

Pure Presence Animal Communication

Set of 6 audio files. Rather than creating the illusion of a "correct" way to communicate, this audio shares insight on how we already do connect and where we might take our connection for both pragmatic and esoteric purposes. The simplicity can be startling. This series and the video complement each other in assisting your awareness and expansion.
Find the series here: http://www.kerrilake.com/purepresence.html

"Like" us on Facebook: www.facebook.com/listenlikeahorse

"There are so many paths to enlightenment that have been taught throughout the eons of human existence, and there has always been the profound being of nature to guide us.

But with every path, with every teaching, there is a time when we are invited to step beyond our teachings, to step beyond the comfort of the systems that supported us, and enter a whole new conversation.

You have the ability to go direct to your own source, and share it, as you wish."

From my heart, this project is in love with everyone.

Especially these ones…

Lydee Scudder
Danielle Hering
Stormy May
Julie Roth
Julie Freeman
Lois Sheppard
Steven Milligan
Montrese Etienne
Colette DeVore
William and Mary Linville
Becci and Bruce Christensen
Monika Broecker
Ambereen Quadir
Jennifer Hough
John and Diane Podkomorski
Tamiel Jones
Cruiser
Navarre
Bernie
Lelu
Mandala
Torch

An Organic Reality happens without trying.

It's what life looks like when we stop trying to be something and stop trying to avoid being something.

Animals live in this reality. They live and express exactly how they feel each and every minute -- their perceptions, preferences and wisdom -- just by being who and what they are.

As we remember that the animals in our lives are creatures of equal value, intelligence and wisdom, we make ourselves available to hear, understand and apply what they have to share.

True equality is the absence of judgment. Throughout our time and activities with animals, they perpetually lead by example: how to live in community, how to let others be exactly who they are, and how to allow ourselves the same freedom.

Listening, hearing and clearly understanding what animals have to share, requires one thing and one thing only, an open heart. As we open our hearts, where no judgment has ever existed, we tap into the language shared by all creatures throughout time and space.

What we hear comes more clearly as we embrace ourselves, accept our own humanity, and know that the entire animal kingdom is here to assist us, to love us, to share and evolve with us, side by side.

Introduction

What I see in people, in humanity, is such beauty, so much capacity for kindness. I also see confusion and doubt that there is any space for that kindness to exist, that it could actually be "the way it is." Watching people argue with each other, watching people fight, even at the age of 3, made me want to stand up and say, "Hey…you guys…there is a different way!"

Horses found me at an early age. As the story goes, while other kids were screaming to be put on the back of a horse for one of those walk-in-a-circle pony rides, I was screaming when they tried to take me off! It was never about riding for me though – it was always about being with the horses. Being in that warm conversation that requires no words and has no evaluation for the correctness of my state of being. The animal kingdom shares that space with us always.

I was born awake and ready to share my perspectives, and in childhood, I learned to not speak, to not share. I learned that when I tell the truth, other people are uncomfortable, and I learned to convince myself that I am no different than any other person.

At first, that was exciting! If I am no different, then everyone else must be able to talk to the animals, too, right? I was able to see the heart, kindness and love in everyone, but they didn't always choose to behave from that place. It can be very confusing to young humans.

How can I communicate with people who are capable of not acting on their own kindness? How do the horses and the animals continue to give to people? These were my guiding questions through my life's journey of embodying all that I am.

There is so much accessible to us in communication with each other and with the animals. There is so much accessible to us in communication with our own higher levels, our higher power, and life as it occurs on many vibrational levels. And there is a growing number of people who are recognizing the opportunity to expand into more. Of course, these are spiritual concepts, inviting humanity to awaken to who we truly are as unique aspects of divinity. That one person doesn't realize they are divinity does not change the truth of who they are.

Whether it's labeled as spiritual or pragmatic, whether it's correct or incorrect, the truth is, the awareness of humanity is expanding. Communication already happens in profound ways that many have been taught to fear, ignore and avoid. But this kind of communication is an integral part of who you are. You are a unique facet of life, included in this communion, included in the benevolence and kindness of sharing our hearts. To step into all that you are may require a new perspective.

In 1995 I was finished with this place. I had learned so completely to hide my truth, that there was no space for my uniqueness. Even with the knowing in my heart, I couldn't find kindness anymore, I couldn't see the beauty, even in the presence of the horses, and I decided to leave. There wasn't going to be anything messy about getting out of my body, I was just going to leave. And I did.

For about a month, I simply stopped living and took myself all the way out of the body. I was met by two presences in the void between physical life and non-physical life, my friends who came to greet me on this part of my journey. I was held in the love that I knew in my heart and reminded why I came into physical life in the first place. We laughed and laughed, and I received more and more information about life here in the physical world. I was reminded why humanity is here doing this dance in the first place. And I was reminded of who I truly am, how much fun there is to be had, and how much I really do love being in a body on a planet.

The stories and writings shared here in this book are communications of kindness. They are doorways to perspectives of kindness that I've walked through as I integrate what I know with how I express it.

You have the capacity to communicate, to express what is true in your heart. The animals are here to assist us, to share in that journey. You've been taught through eons of training and competition that you must earn and prove the viability of your own existence, but this simply is not the truth. When we have the courage to say "no thank you" to what is not the truth in our heart, our outside world begins to change to match what IS in our heart. This is the magic of divinity.

Whether you are already a spiritual healer or teacher or just coming into an awareness that there's a kinder way to be with animals, as you expand your perspective beyond "the right way to be," you create space to become more of who you truly are.

Sharing this writing with you is sharing perspective. There will be tools and guidance along the way that are applicable pragmatically and energetically. Your unique view of what you read, and the way you integrate your own heart into your expression is the real gift. As you embody more of who you truly are, the entire world benefits.

Who you truly are can be sensed, or felt within, through and as your body. The animals assist us to know that unique sensation as we interact with them. You can choose to remain dominant and compete with yourself for control and "rightness," or you can find assistance to expand your awareness of that truth that is unique to you. It happens on a sensory level, the same place where true two-way communication with animals is felt.

With great love, have an awesome journey!

Table of Contents

Listen Like A Horse
Relationships Without Dominance

Cooper

Cooper is a horse. There are a lot of people who know him: trainers, owners, former owners, admirers. One of the cool things about horses is that while many different people can live or work with an individual horse, they can all see different things in the same horse -- and everybody will be right. Horses are like that. They can be anything for those with eyes to see.

Mostly, to me, Cooper is a goofball. He loves to play. Whatever you bring to him, in his world, it's playtime! This can be hard for people to understand, especially when he plays the way a horse plays -- with teeth, hooves, or pushing with shoulders and hips, like a mini-body slam. Cooper is a big guy, with big energy. And he knows how to use it.

"This is where he bucked me off," Lynda told me. "We were trying to get him over his anxiety of being away from the mares. Dan told me to walk him around that manzanita one more time, and we did. When we got to that little hill, my attention when back to Dan for a moment, and all of a sudden, off I went.

"I know it was my lapse of attention, and he took advantage of it. But I can't figure out why he would do such a thing! He doesn't have a mean bone in his body."

Where and when did we all decide that horses have it in for us? That they're trying to take advantage of us? It's so common. People will talk about a horse's behavior like it's personal to us, like their expression is a personal affront to all that we are. In her heart, I see Lynda really doesn't feel that Cooper is deliberately trying to take advantage of her, but there is such an ingrained training for humans to perceive any uncomfortable behavior as an offense, and react with what can be a very punishing defense.

Sometimes people defend themselves with perspective. If we can't make an immediate physical change to the situation, we may adopt a perspective that makes our emotions seems justified. For example, saying that Cooper's behavior of bucking is a bad attitude and needs to be corrected can lead to punishing "training" methods. There is nothing wrong with that perspective, but it can be equally true that Cooper's bucking is a communication of just how uncomfortable he is and this is how he's letting us know. The first perspective may lead to more control and punishment while the second may lead to greater understanding.

Horses sense this. They sense us and they respond to us, even when we don't necessarily know the full extent of what we're communicating.

Of course Cooper picked the precise moment to buck when it would be most effective to be free of doing exercises that stressed his anxiety. He wanted to be with the mares, not working on his anxiety, human-style. It's actually very wise and efficient to find the moment of least resistance to make a change to his situation, which, in this case, was to dislodge the rider who wasn't honoring his requests to be with the other horses. Yes, he absolutely did take the greatest advantage of the timing, but I can't see how this is in any way an offense to Lynda or Dan … totally acknowledging that falling off a horse can hurt in several ways.

Cooper loves playing with people. He loves partnering and sharing his world and how he feels. He will give his entire world. He just wants to be honored and enjoying himself along the way. And this is his gift - to play rather than "work." It is a gift that can be easily misinterpreted by some as "bad behavior."

When I started playing with Cooper, he showed me a lot of stress. He would walk his shoulder straight into me, then turn his head toward me with an open mouth, looking for something to grab in his teeth. Those behaviors in themselves can be pretty intimidating and uncomfortable to be around. I just moved out of the way of his shoulder, no drama or punishment; but the mouth kept coming.

"Dan says you just have to do this," Lynda tells me, showing me how she's been taught to use her elbow to run interference between Cooper's mouth and her body, "and you just put your elbow up every time he wants to swing his head around."

"And how's that working for you?" I asked.

"It really doesn't! He keeps doing it anyway."

"Yeah, and it feels really icky, doesn't it? In your body? Can you feel that harsh feeling of being invaded?"

She shares with me, "You know, it really does feel like that, like he's grinding at my body when he comes at me with his mouth. It's way more uncomfortable than just being afraid I'll get bitten."

This is Cooper's trump card. He knows how to use his energy with people, how to tune his own sense to create emotional discomfort in a person when he swings his head as if he's going to bite. He doesn't actually bite a person's body, although he'll grab a pinch of your clothing. But it is very uncomfortable all the same. He knows it, and he uses it.

"I get tired of just poking my elbow at him, but I don't know what else to do. He doesn't seem to care about being reprimanded or punished, and I don't have the heart to just beat on him for it." Lynda continued to share.

So, I'm listening to all of this, to what the trainers teach, to Lynda's response, and I am feeling the entire communication. I get the visual and sensory downloads of where this behavior was born and how to move beyond it. The foundation underlying all of this is a very simple misinterpretation of Cooper's behavior.

Cooper loves to play. He loves to play with people! In fact, when Cooper is with people, that's all he's doing is playing, like a horse! It looks like teeth, and shoulders and hips and hooves. He's playing with his energy, shoving, insisting, invading, like a horse, but in a human world.

Humans tend to have this mindset of fixing or correcting, as if the horse is doing something wrong by being who he is. We have this mindset that's been developed over eons that a horse needs to be dominated, controlled, trained. We have this fear that if we lose control, if we lose dominance, we will be injured, damaged, or even worse, feel embarrassed. Humans, when faced with embarrassment or loss of control, will often go straight into dominance by whatever means necessary.

Horses aren't out to prove something to us, to prove us right or wrong with what they give or don't give - the horses give from a place of "this is how it feels to be me in this scenario." People may be asking a horse to perform a movement, and this asking may be the only way a person knows how to communicate their heart's desire for connection. The person may not be aware of their deeper wanting. Even when the horse doesn't give the exact movement we're requesting, their efforts are always an attempt to connect with us and share their unique expression.

Through their behaviors and energy, horses will always be expressing who they truly are, even if they are treated so harshly that we'd say their spirit is "broken." Even a broke horse is expressing, "This is who I am when I'm a broke horse."

Energy

Recently my friend Olivia was asking my advice about how to work with a stallion who had not been handled in a very long time. Several people had tried but walked away afraid of this horse. He would bare his teeth, run around, rear up on his hind legs, and throw his body with a sense of intimidation. How do you bring about change in a horse like this when you can't get near him?

I offered Olivia the suggestion that she sit with him, outside his corral, on the hay or something, and just listen to him, share herself with him. He's been cooped up for a long time with nobody to play with. This is not a bad horse; this is a horse with a lot of energy and nobody with the awareness to listen to how he'd like to share it.

It's so common to think we have to train horses, to correct them, to make them into something. This situation isn't an immediate call for training, control or dominance. This is a call for presence without judgment. The truth is, the horse will tell you exactly how to be with him when he has the gift of your awareness. This horse has a lifetime of awareness of people, of his surroundings, of his abilities. He's had people who have dominated and trained him, but until now, nobody who's listened to what he knows, what he is aware of and how that has shaped his world.

The way he communicates may look on the surface like "burning off energy." He can burn his energy by moving his body, breathing, snorting, all the things horses do. He can also move his energy by sharing stories telepathically, sharing his sense of the world, sharing what we call frustration, sadness, and joy. All of those vibrations are stored up in his body - physically, emotionally, spiritually, dimensionally; all of that stagnant awareness can be finally enjoyed in conversation when we listen!

The way we choose to listen may look like "energy work." In both directions, from the horse to the human and the human to the horse, the space that allows the energy to move is our awareness that something is actually available to move. As Olivia put her awareness on listening to him rather than fixing him, he was able to express himself, to share his energy. She didn't evaluate whether it was a "good" way to use his energy or a "bad" way, she just listened as if he was saying, "This is how it feels!"

Olivia's part was to listen, to sense all that he was sharing, and not put it into a box labeled "what a horse is." She sat and listened, all the while knowing, sensing, that being close physically, feeling safe, is what they both wanted. She listened, knowing that once all of this energy moves and transforms, they will be able to stand together for grooming, to exercise, and explore together, and that is exactly how it has played out.

Energy responds to our awareness because that is how the system is designed. That is why we, as creators incarnate, have the ability to create and re-create our outside world through endless methods in the dance with pure consciousness. Ultimately, the question comes down to our motivation. If we are going to create a change in the energy, what causes us to make that change? Where is it coming from? Is it coming from judgment or need? Is it coming from repetition of what we were taught by those who were unaware? Is it coming from the knowing of communion with our heart and all of life?

Energy is a way to describe movement, whether we're talking about movement of physical objects or simply our awareness. What we are moving is Creation. Our awareness is the catalyst to move all of creation, energetically, including mountains!

The best part about this is that we can't get it wrong. The moment we shift our awareness, energy begins moving differently! And when we shift our awareness to be in alignment with the truth of our heart, our energy, the energy in our relationships, our work, our health, and our wealth all align themselves to create the greatest expression from our heart.

There are so many paths to enlightenment that have been taught throughout the eons of human existence, and there has always been the profound being of nature to guide us. But with every path, with every teaching, there is a time when we are invited to step beyond our teachings, to step beyond the comfort of the systems that supported us and enter a whole new conversation. You have the ability to go direct to your own source, and share it, as you wish.

I watched Cooper and his biting games, his shoulder games, his hip and hoof games. I felt him throw his energy into me, that really sickly feeling that makes my insides curdle. But I don't have a heart to be punishing or dominating. Besides, punishment really only works if you want to create a fight -- which I don't. So I kept listening.

One of Cooper's more colorful dances would happen while being walked with a halter and lead rope from his pasture gate to the round pen and back. He would hold back for a moment, then charge forward, bumping the human with his left shoulder, then bolting out ahead as if he'd been spooked. He wasn't spooked. This behavior leaves a person feeling a bit threatened, afraid for their own safety. The horse and the situation feel totally out of control. His game leaves the person with no leverage, no way to use physical force to hold onto him as he is 10 feet out ahead. It's a good trick!

As Cooper's game plays out, the person has let go of the lead rope and he's trotting off to find a nice patch of grass, ready to play chase if you'd like to try to round him up. Such a fun game!

When he is finally collected and re-gathered by a person who may be understandably frustrated, out comes the mouth again, with that feeling of intensity that just makes your skin crawl. What is this behavior and how do we interrupt it? Do we just work it out of him? Crack a whip? Make him run until (we hope) he realizes that if he does what we want he can stop running?

That's one way to do it. It's common. It's a lot of work though. It can feel like punishment to both horse and human, and it's a perpetual fight for dominance. This is what Cooper was expecting from me -- his resistance, his challenges, his every response told me that this was one of the ways he knows horses and people can be with each other.

That approach really doesn't work for me, in my heart. I've tried it! After all, that approach is sort of the foundation of "training," along with the perspective that the horse needs to show respect, to submit, to become what a human thinks he should be. And every time I tried to act that dominant way, I felt I was betraying myself, trying to be something I'm not in order to make him into something he's not.

Instead, I show him a different perspective. How can I listen to him without judgment or punishment? Simply asking that question creates new space to start hearing each other, seeing each other, and sensing so much more together.

Listening is what happens when we stop analyzing ourselves and our lives and open up to what else is there...

Bridging Perspectives

From shamanism to scientific behavior study and the everyday connection with our pets and therapy animals, there are many different ways to talk about the communication between people and animals. For the past 30 years, the practice of Animal Communication has grown as a very spiritual practice, bringing awareness to the sentient nature and multi-dimensionality of the animal kingdom. The language that is used in spiritual realms can seem very esoteric and is sometimes rejected by people who just aren't familiar with it. The information that is available though, can be used in very pragmatic ways when we can hear the language without judgment.

The people who show up as healers and communicators play the role of translators of this esoteric information. All of the information that animals share with us is relevant. Being open to it is really no different than being open to a new conversation with a new friend from a different walk of life. We can be open and listen without judging what we hear, or we can judge and evaluate the information, comparing it to what we think is "right." Neither way is better than the other, but each approach produces very different experiences and awareness.

There is a great difference between judgment and clarity, especially when we request information that comes through esoteric means like animal communication. For example, "Okay, now that I know my horse enjoys white flowers, how will that help us win the futurity?" or, "my dog barks incessantly. Knowing that she sees different dimensions doesn't necessarily make my neighbors stop complaining." If that kind of information brings frustration or judgment, we may want to ask for clarity or for more information. The questions invite further information for how to ask new questions and how to use the clarity we get. It all changes when we start listening to the animals beyond our common knowledge of training or teaching.

Judgment sounds like this: "He should know that I don't need him to bark incessantly. Tell him his anxiety is a waste of all of our energy." or, "My horse has been down that trail a hundred times - she should know I won't let anything happen to her."

These opinions are totally valid, and there is nothing wrong with them. But going forward in this frame of mind is creating judgment after judgment. It leads to a journey of battles, trying to prove our rightness, rather than invite communication. Judgment leads to fixing problems rather than creating effective and elegant responses.

And the amazing beauty of it all is, no matter if we are judging, listening or otherwise, the animals will say to us, "As you wish."

Emotions

Have you ever gone to a dinner party or some other gathering with a friend or family member, and when you arrive, you are feeling great -- everything is going well, people are enjoying each other. But for some reason, you start feeling this sense of frustration and resentment. You start feeling emotional and you want to leave. It gets more intense, and you really don't want to be there, but you really don't want to disrupt what appears to be a group of people enjoying each other.

Eventually, your hints and suggestions work, and it's time to go. You get in the car and there is this tension hanging there. You want to say something about it, but it is so strange and you don't know where it came from ... it doesn't make any sense ... that emotion doesn't even feel like it came from you! How can that be?

Our range of emotion is so dynamic that it not only includes emotions generated by our own judgments, it also includes the ability to sense and embody the emotions of others. How talented we are!

What are emotions, anyway? What creates them? What is their source? What is it in our world that invokes the energy of emotion?

There have been and are so many times when I'm with a horse and I begin to feel frustration, sadness, or happiness for that matter. I let it run its course on a sensory level. I watch the sensations in my body, and sometimes there will be pictures that come with it, something from the past that didn't go the way I wanted it to, something from the future that I've decided must turn out in a particular way, another person who did not meet my expectations, a memory of an interaction I wish would happen again. The scenarios are endless. And the emotions have nothing to do with the horse in front of me. They have everything to do with my decision on an emotional level that this is "the way it should be."

For a long time now we, meaning humans, have been bringing our awareness to our emotions, honoring emotions as an aspect of who we are. It has been a wonderfully enlightening invitation to step out of the dark ages and treat each other with compassion. The idea that others have feelings similar to our own, and having the courage to let others feel what they feel, has served our societies and our awareness by demonstrating that we are certainly not alone in this world. Emotions have been used as a basis to build relationships, to know ourselves more intimately, to have a common language between individuals who live intimately together and much more. Emotions have also been used, for a very long time, to manipulate one another and ourselves.

If something is "good," then we can feel "happy." If something is "bad," then we can feel "upset." If something happens that "shouldn't have" happened, then we can be "angry." If something happens that is "righteous and justified," then we can feel "proud." Can you see a common thread here? Each emotion requires a judgment, an opinion. Without an opinion, why would there be an emotion? Without an opinion, everything is what it is, and we get to dance with it all, without having to defend why it is "good" or "bad," why we "like it" or "don't like it." All emotion is a direct result of a judgment, and the range of judgments is endless!

Now, here is a question for you: Is judgment "bad"?

We can exponentially complicate our emotional state by compounding our judgments. Isn't that awesome? When we begin judging judgment, that it is "good" to know that judgment is "bad," for example, we give ourselves so many more combinations of emotions to dance with. It's not a bad thing, it's not a good thing. It's just how it works.

The animal kingdom is not in judgment, which contributes to why they are so therapeutic for humanity. The animals are not carrying the charge of evaluation or judgment -- that is our game exclusively, and it is part of the divine uniqueness of humanity that lets creation be so diverse.

People are realizing and honoring the emotional range of the animal kingdom as well. The animals absolutely feel the same range of emotions we feel, but there is a significant difference. In the animal world, they are not creating the emotional charge through judgments that life can be good or bad. They are responding to and communicating the vibration of emotion that produces different recognizable sensations. We then assign emotional labels to the sensations.

Animals do feel the loss of those who are close. They feel a magnetic disconnect when a loved one dies. Their heart, body and soul are affected when their connections change. Yet, they are not judging. They are expressing, "this is how it feels to be me as this is going on."

As we truly embody all that we are, we necessarily transcend emotions, because we transcend judgments. We've been taught that our emotions are part of what makes us who we are, and that is true ... until it's not.

Becoming A New Perspective

Lynda gave me her blessing to play with Cooper, to invite him into a different perspective and a different way of being. So, I showed up as a different way of being.

In his early days, Cooper had been with people who interpreted his type of playing as bad behavior. They offered to "correct" his behavior, which was called "training." The actions to correct the behavior had far less impact than the energy and emotion behind them.

Cooper really uses his energy of invasion when he plays the mouth games. He knows how to activate emotional energy, and people often respond defensively. When people respond defensively, it can look pretty offensive, like punishment, hitting, yelling, and generally forceful retaliation that gets justified as "correction."

A horse receives this kind of correction and punishment like a horse would receive any other being, as if the communication is saying "this is who I am in this scenario." In our mind we are saying, "You stop that behavior because I don't want to get hurt." What a horse receives is, "You are telling me who you are. This is what people do. This is how to behave with people."

So here's Cooper, in his early days, trying to engage and play with people because that's who he is. The people interpret the invasive energy as dominance and try desperately to "correct" him, to assume a dominant position over the horse. The horse, who wasn't trying to be dominant but was simply interacting in his terms, learns that when he invites play from people, this is how people play -- roughly. "If I use my face and move to bite at them, they will play along, and they like to play roughly. If I use my shoulder, we get to engage more. We get to play the running-chasing game." He wasn't necessarily looking to dominate or be dominated, he was just being who he is.

As a new perspective, rather than assume that he is out to get me, that he is trying to dominate me and control me, I open my heart and my listening differently. There is nothing in the truth of my heart that says this horse wants to hurt or own me, even though the concept of dominance is what is taught. My heart knows there must be a different purpose behind his behavior. So I ask Cooper, "What is it you are wanting? What is it you are trying to get out of people when you use your invasion, your mouth, your shoulder?"

I don't look for an accurate answer from him. I look for the answer in my own senses.

You see, the human mind likes to look to the outside world for answers. That way, it can compare what it sees to what it already knows and determine a plan of operation in any given environment. Often, the mind won't allow forward movement until it feels it has a good plan, tested and researched, that seems to lead to what it thinks it wants. A mind can want complete analysis before anything may be approved as a reasonably worthy endeavor. The mind is the one that dominates, punishes, and controls... judges. It's not a bad thing, it's not a good thing. It's just the way most minds have been programmed.

The mind can be very powerful and use techniques that are effective at control but not necessarily effective at relationship. Or understanding. Or clarity of the heart.

I had no plan. When Cooper threw his invasion energy at me, I listened, not with my ears, but with my body. The tension, relaxation, breathing, and other subtle sensations in the body speak volumes when we are available to listen. As I felt the energy of those senses in my body, I watched the images that appeared in my mind.

The images that came through were of Cooper being handled by humans the way many foals are handled when they are halter trained. Young horses often have their entire body restrained in order to make them walk or move where we want them to go. During this restraint, a halter may be fastened on the young horse's face. Sometimes people hold the young horse's tail and use it as leverage to get the young horse to move. There are times when the young horse resists this kind of handing and the resistance can look like the young horse is fighting and wrestling.

The images I saw were of humans with Cooper who interpreted his behavior as "bad" or "inappropriate." I see Cooper struggling to understand how to play with people in this sort of "game" they brought to him. I see him playing back in a more aggressive wrestling manner. The humans respond to his exaggerated behavior with stronger "wrestling" behavior, some straps and other gadgets (i.e., a halter on his face and a lead rope). Cooper resists and plays the game again, but this time he isn't able to move freely. He is wrapped up with straps and gadgets. There is an emotional energy that we would label "frustration," and Cooper learns that this energy is part of the dance with people. It feels less like people are there to engage with him, less available, less fun, and the connection with them disappears.

Cooper is so happy to play with the people, but what he wants is the connection, "I'm right here! Let's be friends!" So he starts the play behavior the humans showed him -- wrestling-play. The humans interpret this as "bad behavior" and respond with punishment, control and dominance, without listening. Cooper waits for his next opportunity to play, happy to play rough if that is what the people want to do. This is a story he tells me began for him from a very early age.

As I listen with my heart, I feel that through all of it, he's just asking to be friends, to feel connected, to express who he actually is.

I could doubt myself at this point, question whether or not I just made up that whole story, which is what many people do. But what good does it do for me to doubt what I sense and feel? What good does it do to my friendship with Cooper to analyze whether or not I should open my heart to his world when I could simply let it be true that halter-training was a rough endeavor for him?

Through an intricate journey of control, fear and misinterpretation, the people taught him how to be with people -- roughly. Is it a "bad" thing? That the people's behaviors were rough?

Over the years, through his "training," Cooper developed many ways to be with people. He learned that certain behaviors and responses created harmony, and participating in harmony is generally what welcomes a connection with people. To people, this looks like "good behavior." But who he is, and what he learned about people early on was still there – people are available to play rough, and if it seems like people aren't in connection with him, Cooper can always go back to being rough.

Interrupting A Rough Perspective

If I'm going to show up with Cooper as a different way, as a different and congruent perspective, then I need to be really clear about what I'm bringing to the conversation.

How can I be with a horse who is often rough with me, without being rough back? How can I be with him in a way that he will notice the difference and have the freedom to join me if he chooses? How can I be in his presence so that he knows we can ride together, walk, graze, groom and dance together without a battle?

I learn how to embody the communication of, "Thank you, but no thank you." No fighting, no battle, no dominance, no submission.

This became my presence when he faced me with behaviors that don't work in my world. I don't enjoy rough wrestling with horses, because my human body just won't hold up to it. When it's time to go be with Cooper, my response to his roughness was "thank you, but no thank you." I simply refused to play without making the statement that this kind of play is "bad." This is where the nuances of communication can get confusing for people. But the awareness of these nuances is what communicates congruently.

Refusing to play can seem obvious: we can leave the paddock, we can make him work rather than putting up with his games, we can close ourselves off to him, take our connection away, or we can close our hearts and punish him.

Becoming the space of "thank you, but no thank you" is none of these things. It is being very connected with him with an open heart, and finding no fault in his behaviors. It is not engaging an invasive face, and at the same time, not ignoring the face. It is the willingness to step outside of training regimen to stand next to a horse and, in effect, let him "win" without endangering myself physically. The "win" in this situation is that he gets to express himself without being punished. My awareness of what I sense is what keeps me safe without having to dominate his behavior.

If I let it be true that he is doing his utmost to instigate connection and not dominance, then I will also let it be true that nothing he does is an intentional affront to me. Not one thing about it is personal to me, about me, or against me, and I have nothing to defend against. I do, however, have freedom to engage the battle or not engage.

Sometimes not engaging does mean stepping out of a round pen, or a paddock, but it does not mean disconnection or removing my heart. In fact, when I step out, I actually open myself further, expand my connection further, amplify it so he can feel me, so I can feel him. Our hearts are still connected, but I'm not interested in playing the rough face game. Thank you, but no thank you.

One of the first times I led him out from his pasture toward the round pen, he had all sorts of games for me. One of them was striking at me with his front hoof. Now, as a human, I have a response to that for my own sense of safety. I don't remember exactly what I did. I wish I had it on tape, actually. But I'm confident I let out a loud "HEY!," which is pretty standard for me. I likely stood up very tall in front of him, raising the vibration of my own presence to "impenetrable."

In my energetic field, I began a new conversation and vibration. I became aware of my newly recharged truth: "That behavior is unacceptable in my presence." In other words, just as another horse may communicate "don't come near me" while simply standing still, the communication of my presence is now there for him to sense. Humans have all of the ability and capacity to communicate on those sensory levels, no matter how much experience we have or don't have with horses. It is simple, natural, sensory communication, and humans are as natural as nature.

After he tried that hoof game with me, and I re-tuned my own conversation, we still needed to get to the round pen. I could remain angry, charged and emotional about it and punish him by removing my connection and my heart. But I couldn't figure why I would want that battle. So, letting out a breath as if it never happened, because why would I want to invite that behavior back into my world by holding onto it, we walked forward into the round pen and shut the gate behind us.

Being kicked at wasn't very much fun for me. It's a very intense feeling when a horse strikes at you with a front leg. The sense of bodily danger brings a shot of adrenaline, and adrenaline just isn't my favorite drug.

The key to becoming a different perspective is to be always moving forward, no matter what the pace. Forward "fixes" everything. Will we go forward in battle or into a new space?

Many people don't realize that holding onto an old event, retelling the story of a previous behavior, a history of difficulty, can feel in an animal's world as if we are perpetually bringing that discomfort back. The animals are immersed in mental pictures of what we did or didn't enjoy, and they are immersed in our sensory memory of what we did or didn't enjoy. In an animal's world, that immersion can be interpreted as the vision of what we are asking of them, a sense of who we "are" in that scenario. They respond without analysis or judgment, and give us what we are requesting on the subtle levels of awareness, which can result in a repeat of this memory, or behavior, or difficulty, based on how it felt.

So, after Cooper strikes out at me, and I shift my own conversation to include "I honor how you feel, but that behavior isn't acceptable in my presence," we move on. To be honest, I barely have a memory of it -- sharing the event with you here is almost a re-creation of the sensory experience rather than a memory.

When we retain memories, we mostly retain an emotional stamp of what happened. The images can change, our "memory" can change, but the charge of emotions stays pretty consistent, or it gets more intense, until we let it dissolve.

Holding on to the emotional memory and replaying the vision of the event in our minds is no different than telling our horses that this is still a reality we're interested in repeating. The horses may either respond by reproducing that event, or creating a different outcome that feels the same emotionally. They can also learn to ignore the images and sensory communication we express if and when our actions are not congruent with what they sense.

Dissolving the emotions can seem hard, and through years of experience with no other options, we've been convinced it's hard. Emotions are compelling and sticky, but they will actually dissolve easily in the presence of awareness and love. Even with high emotions of being kicked at by a horse, when I return my awareness to my true conversation - being a different perspective - the strength of the emotion pales in comparison to the elegance of connection.

Without denying the emotions, I can see them for what they are -- a natural result of the judgment that being kicked is "bad." Of course, getting kicked would cause pain and a change in how I function, which is not preferable or complementary in my world. But I'm not going to make a big fight out of proving a point. At this point in my conversation with Cooper, my heart and my interest are in moving forward into new space rather than visiting, revisiting, analyzing and protecting myself from the past.

With Cooper, and with any other horse in a situation like that, I let the image, the emotional charge, and the adrenaline dissolve without resistance. He is so adept at using his energy with humans that my showing up as a different perspective, a different way of being, releases the emotional charge and invites him to engage with me on a different level.

Listening Through Resistance

Once we're in the round pen, he lets me know he's been there before. He lets me know that he can play a rough game in there too, that people have played a game of "I can make you do it" in the round pen. He tells me the story through his resistance.

I ask him to walk forward. He says, "I know this game. You ask, I resist, you ask more, I resist more."

I ask him what that's all about, and he shares that this is how he learned it.

The message through the images I get seems simple to me. He is sharing how he interpreted the "training" people offered him. While being totally well-intended, there was an emotional aspect to the training he received… emotions from the people.

Inviting this horse into a new perspective was going to mean having zero dependence on emotions to communicate with him. It doesn't mean elimination of emotions, or denying myself what I feel. But it does mean that if I have to use frustration to motivate him, or anger, or if I become stuck in sadness, or even stuck in happiness that he responds to me, I will have re-embodied the conversation that created his "resistance." Motivation through emotional means would re-invite the use of mouthy behaviors, shoulder pushing, hip throwing and energy invasion. My emotional response is what invites him to come searching for my participation the way he learned people like to play.

With individuals, regardless of species, who naturally have high awareness, high intelligence, or even something intangible that makes them very available to connect, so often their attempts to connect can be perceived as invasion. Their connection can feel like a challenge to our personal world, as if their way of being in the world must be controlled and tempered. What's often happening is that they are seeing us, connecting with us on levels we may not be totally aware of ourselves.

People can use force to control horses at a young age, to teach them to do what we want, whether it's what the horse wants or not. There is nothing wrong with using force -- it is generally a pretty effective way to communicate power over another. Horses will, by and large, bend to that power. But horses like Cooper, who leads with his heart and wants nothing less than full participation in all of life, will still communicate how he sees the world. Whether it's through energy or behavior, he is communicating how it feels to be himself in any given interaction. We can choose to dominate him and "silence" his expression, or we can listen differently. He presents an amazing opportunity for us to become aware of how we see our own world.

When I feel that icky energetic feeling, I don't try to hide from him. He sees right through me anyway. At first, as we started playing together more often, he would give me his face -- he'd just shove his face, his jaw, his neck, right into my space with that sickly feeling of invasion. It feels horrible, so I tell him out loud, "That feels really gross," and I simply move away from his face toward his shoulder. I just groom his hair. It's March and he's starting to drop his winter coat. It's that time of year when being with horses means hairs in your mouth, covering your clothes, and sometimes a stray horse hair in your eye. It's just true!

He brings his head around to me again and offers to grab my sweatshirt with his teeth.

"No thank you," I say out loud. Saying the words out loud sometimes helps me be congruent in the sense of my communication. In my space, what is true for me is that I am a "no-thank-you" to that behavior. So, I feel that truth, without apology, without attack, without punishment, without any charge at all. It's just true. And feeling that truth in my body totally diffuses that icky feeling from his mouthy behavior, almost instantly.

He tries again. After all, it's usually pretty easy to get people to play when you push on them like this! When you push on them, they will swing their arms at your head, just like another horse would swing his face. Sometimes people will interact with hitting, sometimes yelling, and lots of other entertaining behaviors. It's can be pretty easy to get people to engage when you push on their emotions!

But here I am, as a different way of being, as an invitation to his relaxation, and his knowing that he is not alone. I am a presence that connects with him without the need to invade me for a response, without pushing me for a reaction. And he can relax a bit, feel himself a bit more, even though he's not instigating something.

We dance together like this during grooming, as we walk from gate to grass, from grass to hay, from hay to round pen, from round pen back to herd. He is such an interesting guy. He wants so much to be busy, to share a job to do. And let's get that straight. It's not that he needs a job to do, it's that he loves sharing a job to do. Life is more fun and interesting with a partner! And he's happy to be what his partner needs, to complement his partner entirely. But if his partner truly wants to be complemented, it helps immensely for that partner to be open to communicating from the heart. Otherwise, Cooper's actions can be interpreted as "bad behavior."

It's easy to make it the horse's fault. To say that "he should know better by now." The truth is, he does know! It's not that he's trying to be "bad" or "wrong." It's not that the people have been "bad" or "wrong." It's that the people have been unaware of their actual communication, what they have been bringing to the conversation.

Understanding Ourselves

There has been a beautiful movement in the horse world to awaken people to the language and interactions between horses. We've used our observations to start to listen and communicate with horses differently, using what we can see of their language. It's been a monumental awakening that so many have embraced, and many have fought as well. Of course, I'm talking about the horse whispering and natural horsemanship paradigms.

When we endeavor to speak the language of the horse, though, to become one who communicates like a horse, we start trying to listen as if we are a horse. We actually put ourselves in a position to miss how horses respond to humans! We are, after all, humans, not horses.

Our energetic expression is different, our awareness is different, our responses, and our ability to hide the truth from ourselves. All of this is very different than horses. Communion with another cannot happen without acknowledgment of uniqueness. When we are available to embrace our own humanity, we are then available to be embraced by the unconditional love of the animals. We also become available to sense their true communication, the two-way communication that is part of our very nature.

I was so blessed to have about two weeks with Cooper where I was the only person interacting with him. I got to feed breakfast and dinner, and grain! It feels so wonderfully satisfying to share food with my friends like that.

There are little grasses in their pasture, but not enough to sustain the horses. Some days I had thoughts about how the horses are confined and dependent on a person to deliver a substantial amount of food. I found myself thinking whether it is right or wrong to keep horses in this way...and then I woke myself up! How could it possibly be right or wrong?

When I was younger, I started asking the horses how they do it. I asked them directly, "How can you keep giving to people, working for people, showing up as a species to serve and carry people wherever they are asked to go?" And the answers I received, the love I felt still overwhelms me. The horse, as a species, has a consciousness that is so in love with humanity, so available to be of service to our evolution, that the apparent suffering of individuals pales in comparison to the service to the whole. It is no mistake that horses have carried humanity through wars, plowed fields, been inspiration for art, love, power, beauty, and lived as one of the greatest instruments of our forward growth. Horses, as a species, love being in partnership with Humanity.

I can look at horses as victims of humanity if I want to. I can see them as innocent creatures, every single one of them, who have no say in what people do with them, or to them. Often, on an individual basis, that can be true - people often choose to totally dominate animals. But then I look from a different perspective, a bigger perspective.

These horses, all horses, have shown up to participate with people. Their presence is an opportunity not only to know ourselves more completely, but to also know each other, to know the unconditional nature of communion with another life. Many people exchange dollars for horses, but equating the life of a horse with dollars is neither the full story nor the truth of the heart. It's simply convenient.

The awareness and consciousness of horses is as instrumental in bringing them together with us as driving a truck and trailer to a different piece of land, loading a horse in the trailer and driving back. The animals are creating their world right alongside of us -- how many people know a story that sounds like, "You and this horse were destined to be together..."?

Even when an animal is being misunderstood or treated harshly, how can we say it is any less divine, unless we are judging humanity? How can living with horses in this way, that way, or any other way be "wrong?" It's just not possible. The truth of the matter is, Cooper and his mares have found their way here, into Lynda's care, sharing life with her and the rest of us who also show up to play. If we truly want to extend equality to the animal kingdom, let's honor that they have a role in creating their circumstances. From there, if we want to find fault or approval in the horses' circumstances, can we consider that the judgment of their situation is our own and not the horses judging us?

Some people still keep horses in some very uncomfortable conditions. There are rescue organizations and kind people everywhere who do show up to remove horses and other animals from conditions that don't complement their total health and well-being. But the horses are in those situations, too, by divine order. Being in those situations, and being seen by people who know that more is possible is part of what wakes people up to a whole new paradigm.

Those who are not aware of a new paradigm, those who are very entrenched in a system of dominance, greed and control are still very worthy of the horses' presence in their lives. The proof lies in the fact that they actually do have horses in their lives. If this is the only opening they have in their world to be in the presence of horses, to feel, even for a moment that another being on the planet will partner with them, then the horses have done their job. The rest of it is details, even if it includes pain, hunger, hardship. Horses assist humanity to know that we are loved and supported - if another person is not aware of this truth, that is okay. I'll be aware of it for them until they remember.

Does The Horse Love Me?

Feeding the horses takes on a whole new perspective once we have the awareness that the horses have a say in the creation of their own world. The horses are, understandably, in ready anticipation of the hay being presented on their side of the fence. It's been hours since they've chewed and swallowed a whole mouthful! Hours since the blissful meditation of head-down breathing and chewing, swallowing, shifting weight, breathing, chewing, swallowing. I can't even really call it meditation - it's just being who they are when the food is there!

Does this mean the horse loves me? Because I bring them their food? Is this the only reason they love me and perform for me? Does food actually have anything to do with love?

I watch a lot of people beat themselves up on this one. They equate food with love, which actually has very little to do with love. Food is love, in the unconditional sense that all of life is love. But feeding a horse does not mean that the horse now loves me, or that the horse will interpret the presence of food as my love for him.

"If I feed my horse regularly, maybe he'll love me and do what I ask." This is all about approval, not about love. "It will be good because I fed him, so I know he loves me. Then I can accept his good behavior, knowing I earned it by loving him."

The horses aren't keeping score.

When we feed our horses, other animals, or the people in our lives, we may be feeling our love for them while we prepare and serve and share the food. The food takes on the vibration of our love, and tastes better that way! To say that the horse loves me because I feed him is really, really shortchanging our connection and communion with another. Our horses love to feel that vibration of our love, and if getting us to bring the food opens up that love connection, they are SO happy to be there for it!

In Cooper's world, food is love only in the perspective that all of life is the vibration of love. The only way that food has anything to do with people is that people deliver it in red buckets, and not often enough. And who cares what color the bucket is! "I eat here. You put the food in this feeder for me. Unless Emma (one of the mares) shows up, and I get out of her way. Then put the food here so I can eat it. I'm ready!"

Our mind can do backflips in this situation, so to clarify:

"Does Cooper love me?" ...Yes. Unreservedly.

"Would he stop loving me without the food?" ...Absolutely not.

"Would he love me if I didn't feed him?" ...Without question.

"Would not feeding him affect his health and ability to connect and partner and share with me?" ... Undoubtedly, but not because he doesn't love you.

"Will he love me more if I feed him more, or more often?" …
In horse world, this question does not compute.

What we're really asking is, "Would I feel my own love more
if I fed him more or more often?" … If the answer to that is
yes, then Cooper will be more than happy to play his role and
eat more often. That way he can feel and watch my own love
expand; he's happy to eat more anyway, and feeling the love
expand in me is like adding gravy.

I have to clarify here that in this kind of scenario, "love" isn't
really what we're talking about. What we're really talking
about is approval. How much would I approve of myself if I
fed him more or more often? How much would I approve of
my ability to provide, to share, to offer the life-sustaining needs
of another? How much would I approve of myself that I did
something that can make the horse happy?

Conversations With Cooper

The more Cooper and I dance together in a new conversation, the more we step together into a different way of being. It's not about training or re-training him. He's already trained. Training requires acknowledgment of one step, and that is recognition that I'm asking for something. Once the horse, or dog or fish or plant, for that matter, recognizes that I am communicating with them, training is all done. Everything from that point on is a conversation. Either we know what we're bringing to the conversation or we don't. Or, we're confused, which is often the case.

Breath

Breath is such a pure form of communication, chemically, vibrationally, spanning all senses. It has pristine congruency when we let it happen without trying to control it. And the best part is, it's effortless! The body will breathe exactly how it needs to without our conscious control, 100% of the time!

In a herd of horses, breath is an integral part of their communication. An exhale can change the tone of an entire herd. Some exhales are forced, saying, "Hey! Watch out!" Some exhales say, "Oh yeah, this is good!"

Some exhales are cleansing, shaking off a stressful moment. Of course, many exhales are simply clearing the lungs in natural rhythm. Everyone in a herd feels the exhales. Everyone listens to, or senses, the tone of the herd members, their essence, through their breath.

I've shared with so many people that you can work and communicate with a horse with nothing more than your breath, when you are aware of and congruent with what your breath brings to the conversation. The sensory exchange communicates far more than a linear thought. Humans are sensitive to this level of communication, too. The magic comes when we are congruent through each aspect of communication.

What's so entertaining is, so many people, when they get near horses will actually hold their breath in response to fearful anticipation. That anticipation has nothing to do with the horse in front of them! The horse can feel the withdrawal of fluid communication, the contraction of our presence into fear and defense. Our defense leaves the horse to guess at what we are truly asking, and she or he might show us "bad behavior"; what we call "bad behavior" can actually be their attempts to find leadership, to escape or to create relief from the tension.

Humans have the capability to use breath deliberately - to take ourselves to various states of consciousness, to alter the state of our mind or our body. Which is great fun and can be an awesome tool when we realize we haven't been breathing!

But what I really love is when we let our breath be totally honest, totally real. It really doesn't matter what we're accomplishing with our breath as we just let the body breathe, the way that best complements the body.

Our breath is an expression of our truest, greatest contribution in life, our essence. As we let our body take care of the breathing, our breath, on energetic, chemical, auditory, sensory and multidimensional levels says "this is the sense of me right now," to the whole world entirely.

Cooper became fully trained the first time he was handled by people. He was trained that people will push on him, pull on him, invade him and engage in a dance of sometimes forceful interaction. Is this a good thing? Or a bad thing? That's up to you, if you want to judge. In a horse's world, it's just the way it is.

After understanding how people want to be with him, he has had a lifetime of creative interactions where people would show up with different stories, personal histories that had earned their approval or were in battle with themselves over. With each person in every situation, Cooper was just being Cooper, saying to every request, "Okay, I hear you, I'm happy to give, and this is how it feels to be me in response to this situation."

All horses are masters of emotion, simply by being who they are. How they communicate their response to emotion varies widely and is often misinterpreted. If the horses are showing us a behavior in response to our own emotions, and we act on it without listening, we may go straight to dominance, correction and punishment. Behavior in response to emotions can be really, really uncomfortable for us. We can sometimes redirect the energy the horse was expressing in response to emotion, or it can be squelched and silenced in dominance.

There are some individuals who have a level of awareness, we might call it an intelligence, although it is an awareness, and a heart that will not allow itself to be dominated. Their expression will continue to show up no matter how much we try to train it out of them, so to speak.

One of the ways people have begun talking about the emotional interactions between horses and humans is to say that horses are a mirror for us. The very aware, gifted horses will often show up with people who are listening on this level because their communication is more likely to be heard and not corrected as if it is "bad behavior."

To say that horses are mirrors for us is a beginning. If I were to look at Cooper only as a mirror for myself, though, I would miss his uniqueness. To look at his behavior as a straight representation of me, I could be interpreted as a human who enjoys conflict, who feels unheard and has found a way to survive in that environment, who has explosive energy and isn't always sure what to do with it, who responds unexpectedly at times to unclear communication. And the truth is, if I go looking for it, I can find all of that in myself, to be sure.

Seeing these things, I can look to correct myself. I can begin to work at uncovering the history, the story behind what would produce those traits in myself. I could do that -- I'm open to seeing it, because it is a beautiful doorway to seeing more than is on the surface.

I could also be looking for stories and histories that explain Cooper's behavior based on what other people have programmed into his interactions. But stepping into a new perspective has nothing to do with history and stories.

My questions change, and I want to ask, "What else is there? How do I know that this is me and not him, or even the other people he's been with in his life?" What I really want to know is, where is Cooper's heart, the part that is free of what others have projected onto him and pressured him to be?

When we meet a horse who shows up with "behavior problems", we're not really dealing with just that individual horse. We are dealing with the programming that previous humans set into place in their interactions with this individual horse. All behavior is "fixable" or "changeable." All anxieties are reachable, when we are available to see the horse separately from the people and circumstances of the past. As I am able to be with a horse, knowing that his world truly has nothing to do with me, this is the foundation of all healing - the ability to sense and acknowledge the truth of the individual upon whom various untruths have been stacked. It's not personal.

Cooper started showing me the intricacies of the conversation he's been in with humanity. He kept inviting me into a battle, a struggle of "You have to make me" or "you can't make me." I simply didn't play along, and at the same time, I didn't abandon him. He'd move away, I'd move with him without calling it good or bad.

The general belief is that you have to correct a horse who behaves that way, who walks away, who moves his body differently than he's been directed. You need to make him know that he is to stand still. If he moves, you bring him back to the place where he is to stand, and you begin again. Some people would include a punishment in there, in the form of a hit or a jerk on the lead rope. They may deliver that punishment out of a sense of not knowing what else to do, repeating what the trainer did, or a sense that this is what another horse would do. None of it is wrong, and the horses love us no matter what. The corrections and punishments are a form of communication delivered in dominance. To be truly effective in communication, not just dominant, it helps to know what we want to be saying to the horse before we ever ask for anything.

The perspective that I was bringing to him, the way I was being, was to say to him, "I will not fight you, I will not trap you (other than having him tied, which can actually be quite a trap when you look at it), I will not punish you and I will not invade you. But I also will not be intimidated. I will not be exasperated, I will not pity you, nor will I diminish myself. I will be right next to you."

That is my state of being through our interactions. My state of mind is open to something new, something I haven't seen before. The state of my heart is welcoming of all that occurs, without judgment.

As I groom him in this state, he may, almost reflexively, bring his mouth to my clothes, to nip or push me. But somehow, he just seems to have no energy for it anymore. You can see it in his eyes, as if he is aware that he's used to playing that game, but it just doesn't feel the same way. He brings his head part-way around, and almost like he's been distracted, he just ceases that behavior. He relaxes, licks his lips, lets out a breath and receives the grooming, which comes with gentleness. I simply groom him in this state of neutrality. I make no fuss over his "good" behavior or that he stopped his "bad" behavior. There is no punishment, no praise, just "thank you" with love in the grooming.

As he opens up to me, I say thank you. It feels very different than saying "good boy." I say thank you. I thank him for his receptivity, I thank him for his touch, for his acknowledgment. I thank him for being next to me, for being a horse I can groom, for being the magnificence he is in my life. He feels it, and he yawns. And in my saying thank you, I realize I am speaking for us both.

Often when we feel like talking around our animals, we are expressing not just our own sense and awareness, but also an awareness that includes what they are feeling or sensing. It's just that we use words for it, which works for us humans. The words I say most often around any animals are, "I love you!" I actually say it around people pretty darned often, too.

"Hello! I love you! Thank you!" Those are the most common words I say. The animals feel them, they feel the tone, the truth in the vibration, and they respond with connection, awareness, acknowledgement. Why? It feels good! The vibration of those words, when they're used in genuine expression feel harmonious, true, good.

And in that expression, I know beyond any doubt that these words represent what's in the animal's heart at the same time. They don't just have love for us, they are love for us, far beyond just having or showing love through recognizable behaviors. They are love for us. As I express the very tender and yet very powerful words, "I love you," I am being vibrationally who I am, who they are by nature. And they feel it. They know it, and this expression, silently or aloud, is one of the most, if not the most, direct, clear and effective way to invite a loving bond with any other creature.

Cooper dances around for a few minutes when I ask him to lift his left hind foot for me to clean it. I follow his dance, just matching him, not pushing him, just matching him without invading him. My conversation is, "I'd love for your foot to be held up briefly so I can clean the dirt from it." He is trying to escape this task, still locked in the magnetic memory or reality of "the way it's always been."

His left hind foot has been held tightly before, until he felt off balance as he tried to pull it away. Humans created a battle by holding onto his foot when he wanted to put it down. This is another common practice intended to teach the horse that pulling away doesn't work, that the human has the power to dominate that foot. Much of the time, the horses will simply be the first to stop fighting and submit to having their foot held. Eventually, the interaction just becomes "the way it is," and we would say that the horse is "trained" to pick his foot up.

The result of that kind of interaction for Cooper, though, undermines trust and causes him to go straight into defense and anxiety when you even think of asking for that hind foot. His behavior looks like he doesn't know how to stand on 3 legs unless he feels that tough resistance holding onto that hoof. He holds his breath, becomes very stiff and prepares to be knocked off balance. He hasn't shown me through images or senses that he ever actually did fall when his hind foot was held up, but he definitely abandons his own senses to an extent and goes straight into defense. That is how stressful that particular interaction has been for him in the past.

He did offer to kick me once, with his right hind foot. It was not nice. I did communicate back with a sharp crack on his hip with my hand, my way in the moment of communicating that kicking at me is unacceptable in my world. Whether my action was right or wrong, I knew that my communication was saying, very plain and simple, "This will not happen in my world." It's not about anger or punishment, just a simple communication.

In my presence and all of my being, I know beyond any shadow of a doubt that I am not available to be kicked. I become that vibration, or in other words, I integrate that truth into my state of being -- I become a presence that does not invite any kind of kick. I'm just not available to it.

Kicking itself is not bad or wrong, in fact, kicking can be very effective communication. It's not that I am right or good. I'm simply not available to be kicked, and I am open to receiving his communication differently. This is a neutral statement that carries no emotional charge, and the horses understand the simplicity of a message like that.

After I delivered my message to him physically, I stepped away for a moment, to change brushes or put something down, and I used that deliberate moment to let out my breath, to dissolve that intense feeling and come back to awareness of my own state of being. I checked in to see if I still have an emotional charge, or if my presence is congruent again with "Thank you, but no thank you. All is well."

Asking for his right hind foot a second time was a different conversation, a different story. I asked, sharing the communication of my presence with him, and he offered his foot. I felt him sharing his truth that he acknowledges my request, although he's still tense about it. He still held his breath. I held his foot with love for less than 20 seconds, and then released it gently to the ground. "Thank you," I offered him. "Thank you, my friend."

And I exhaled.

And he exhaled.

Boundaries

The more you integrate and know yourself as the aspect of divinity that you truly are, the less need or desire you will have for boundaries.

If I show up in front of a horse with a boundary created from my mind's history or projection of a perceived threat, the horse can perceive a tense vibration that communicates the possibility of something imminently dangerous. Even though the boundary is in my own mind, created from something that happened previously or hasn't happened yet, it still communicates the absence of safety. It's not that I am a threat to the horse, but within my body resides the reality of a threat big enough to build walls against, just in case it arrives.

When I am with a horse, especially one who has been treated harshly, abused, neglected or otherwise mistreated, the first thing I do is watch my own vibration to be clear that I've dropped all boundaries, all barriers between my heart and theirs. There is no more powerful stance than full transparency, full vulnerability. I let that horse see every facet of who I truly am and draw his or her own conclusions about my motivations. From there, I use my tools and skills to interact with the horse in a way that honors us both. I know my motivations, the purity in my own heart, and I let the truth of that vibration flow through me, AS me, my presence.

This is not to say that I allow myself to be treated disrespectfully, to be dishonored or harmed in any way. I am well aware of the behaviors and energies I am available to dance with and those I will not engage. But this awareness has nothing to do with creating walls and boundaries. It has everything to do with awareness of my own presence and communication as expressions of my unique truth. And I know that I am unavailable to be dominated by fear. The real key is in knowing that nothing this horse or anyone else is doing is personal. Whatever they have going on is not about me.

As I show up with no barriers, no boundaries, simply expressing the kindness that is my heart, the truth of who I am, I am not in a space of defense, and I am not in a space of offense. This space of neutrality, of Being, is recognized innately by every species.

Equality With Another Species

When you open to sensing more of yourself, you become far more available to be in communication with others. It is this openness of the heart rather than any training or technique, that invites communion. Your expression from the heart is what communicates the uniqueness of all that we are, and invites the expression of others.

You don't have to have a name for it, there is no requirement to be able to speak about it or prove to another person that it exists, that you are "right" or "justified." Just to become aware that your sensory awareness is open is all it takes to "hear" a horse, or another animal. The truth is, your sensory awareness is always accessible unless you turn away from it. The individuals like Cooper, who are so very familiar with people and so very in love with people, are more than happy to share all that they are.

The horses are my good friends. I'm not their mom. They're not my children or servants. They are my friends. Equals to me. Exquisite beings in horse bodies. Cooper is a horse who makes it very easy to see this perspective. He is a horse, to be sure, but his awareness shows so much more. He is a very aware being on the planet who is living as a horse. If you listen to him, with your expanded senses that are alive in each one of us, he shares easily his clarity in the world, about the world, and as himself in his world. The awareness and clarity he shares has the innocence of simple wisdom that humans sometimes aspire to through a lifetime of meditation, and his wisdom and perspective are available to anyone all the time, always, everywhere.

As Cooper shows me his stiffness and anxiety, I just listen to him, listen to how he expresses himself vibrationally, on a sensory level. When I say listen, what I mean is sense. All communication comes as a vibration of one kind or another - vision uses vibrations of light, hearing uses vibrations of sound, touch uses vibrations through the physical body, breath uses vibrations through the throat and air, etc. Our thoughts are vibrations that affect the whole. There are countless other vibrations constantly in our ambient atmosphere. Our bodies are designed and hard-wired to receive them, and when we become available to it, it is our natural state to interact with one another consciously on these levels.

I feel Cooper's vibrational expression, and it can be translated in so many different ways. There is no reason to control it, or try to make the sensory information come as one particular sense more often than another. In fact, any expectation that communication should come in a certain format will limit what the communication can be. The time and effort it takes to make it into something predictable is more than enough to totally cover up the true nature of what is being shared. So the listening/sensing with Cooper becomes a time of fluid interaction, no control, no expectation, no need or desire; it becomes a different perspective that is a knowing rather than a wanting.

I share my communication with him, too. I feel what it is to pick up his feet to clean them. I feel what it is to have it happen without a battle, without struggle, and with everyone breathing in a relaxed way. Maybe our experience today is something different than that feeling, but I know it will happen. I don't want it, I know it. From there, it will take the time it takes. It will look how it looks. I am not available to be injured, I am not available to injure or punish him. "I love you. Thank you."

Our first few days in this conversation, which happened about 7 minutes at a time, he danced around, still entrenched in the old way of being with people. Resistant, elusive, tense, defensive. I don't blame him. He has a lifetime of interactions with people in that kind of vibration. There was always stress, for him and for them. I saw this dance between us as releasing the steam valve of the build up of all of the stress for every stressful interaction he's had in his entire life. When a horse holds his breath, you know there is some heavy defense going on there. What an honor it is to help him release it.

When he stops dancing and stands still, I touch him with an open hand and say, "Thank you, Buddy." I hear him taking his short, staccato breaths after holding his breath while he dances. And my touch says, "I love you." I exhale. He softens.

I ask him for a foot. He says, "No thank you." There is no fight in me. No defense, no offense, no punishment. I stop. 8 seconds go by.

I ask him for a foot, he thinks about it. That's enough for me. "Thank you!" And I stand up and rub his shoulder. 35 seconds go by.

I ask him for a foot, and he thinks about it. That's plenty for me to see. "Thank you!" And I stand up and rub his shoulder. He lets his breath out. Takes a short breath in. Another 35 seconds.

I ask him for a foot, he thinks about it, and I stay still where I am, breathing in a relaxed way. He shifts his weight. That's enough for me. "Thank you!" And I stand up and rub his shoulder. About a minute has passed. That's enough for today. His hoof will be fine with some poop in it for another day.

At this point, I have all the time in the world to dance this loving dance with him. There is no medical urgency, and we're not running late for our first Olympic performance. So I stop sooner rather than later, ending this part of the conversation early, with love, with him wondering why we haven't had a battle yet. He relaxes his jaw, works his mouth and licks his lips, breathing.

Without the battle, I untie him, and he watches me. He offers no mouth games, no teeth, no invasive energy or shoulder pushing. I offer no effusive praise, no commands, no treats, no high voice, no gruff voice. It's simply time for what's next, and together we walk off.

As I take the lead rope from the tie ring, I hold it like I'm holding hands with my friend, and I turn to walk to a nice grazing area. He watches me. My presence still communicates that I'm not available to be injured, and it also communicates that I'm headed toward that patch of grass where some loose hay has also been spread. That seems like a nice place for a horse to be. He watches me and feels my presence, my communication, and he comes with me, no pressure, no coercion, just walking together, holding hands. And the grass is good!

Grounding

When people speak about grounding, I sort of re-translate that into becoming aware of what's actually happening without trying to control it.

Why would I ever become ungrounded? What's really going on with that? Have I left my body? Have I left my mind? Or is it that my mind has taken control of my body and filled it with thoughts, fears, anticipations and analysis, leaving no room for who I truly am?

Horses sense our energetic, emotional and mental states with clarity without us saying a word to them. They sense what's actually going on within us even when we hide from ourselves. Their response is to what they sense. When we see horses with "bad behavior," or if they seem to resist everything we ask, their behavior can be communication that they sense something in us that is incongruent with our outward expression. It can be very much the same with people's "bad behavior," or misunderstood behavior.

When I'm with the horses, I don't try to ground myself. I just get really, really honest with myself. If I'm scared, I don't try to hide it. If I'm unsure, I don't try to hide it. If I just don't want to do what I'm told to do, I'm honest about it, with a further inquiry into what makes me not want to do something. Being this vulnerable to myself, this honest, leaves me open to judgments, opinions. It leaves me open to my own judgments and opinions. But the alternative is to totally abandon what's currently true for me.

"Grounding" to me seems like a lot of work, the way it's taught, especially if we learned that we need a satin pillow and a familiar corner to get it done. The results can be wonderful, feeling more in the body, feeling, for the moment, more present. But it's still an argument between what is, and what we want it to be. My question always was, "Where is that taking me, and why can't I just go there without all of the work?" As it turns out, we can go there without all of the work! It just happens in a different perspective, a different dimension.

If the truth is that I am wrapped in an internal war, and I take a moment to become "grounded," I've given myself a few minutes break from the storm. But I haven't addressed the storm. That storm is an amazing gift, and attempt to get my own attention. I can take breaks from it as long as I need to, until I have the strength, courage and willingness to turn around, look it straight in the eye and say, "Okay...I'm listening."

Being with horses is one of the most catalytic spaces I know to get really honest, to have the courage to face my own storms. When the horses have "bad behavior," I will always have the option to use my tools and equipment to dominate and control them, to make them bend to my will. They will bend, if I push hard enough. But when I notice this sense of resistance, stickiness, defiance, or "I don't want to," I feel all of that resistance through my own body, and I take notice. Resistance is resistance - even though it can feel uncomfortable, it is not a personal statement about who I am. The horses are not judging, and in their presence, we can remember what it feels like to not be judged.

It's not about making it my responsibility or making it my problem - that's a recipe for a whole new full-time job! No thanks! It's about being aware that horses don't tell lies. They are saying to us, at all times, "This is how it feels to be me right now."

When we are caught in a storm and unavailable to listen on subtle energy levels, then the only way they have to communicate with us is through physical actions and signals. It is up to us, if we'd like, to remain aware that there is more going on here than a horse trying to get away with something, trying to make us look bad. A horse's behavior is not an insult to us. It's not personal. It's communication.

When we start having the courage to interact with and listen to our own storms, we begin to realize just how powerless these storms really are. If I can talk to the storm, I have already freed myself from it, and it truly has no power over me. How grounding is that realization right there? How immediate is the integration of my higher knowing through and as my body with that one awareness?

When you stop battling the battles, magic happens. YOU happen. And if you stop for one moment and take a look...You are, actually, grounded.

Several days in a row we have some version of this conversation, until he lets me know that this is now frustrating for him. At first I wonder if it is me that's frustrated or if it's him. Ultimately it doesn't matter. It's time for a change. No problem.

In our last conversation, when I asked for his left hind foot, the really sticky one, he offered no dancing around. He stood still. There was still some tension, a little holding the breath. But when I asked for the foot, he shifted his weight for me right away, and brought his heel off the ground. No sense of ickyness, no energy jabbing - a clear offer that I am welcome to handle his foot. I lifted it gently and cleaned it. His anxiety kicked in pretty quickly, though, and he forced his foot down to the ground. I just let it happen that way.

"Thank you so much, my friend! I love you!" And I rubbed his shoulder, rubbed his chest, which he loves, and moved on to what's next. As I do, everything that just happened dissolves, making space for our next communication.

It's been taught that horses require repetition. It's not true, necessarily. It's what's been taught. There is a big difference in there between what horses require to be able to understand us, and what we think they require to be able to understand us. The key is whether or not we truly understand what we are asking for.

Once a horse understands that we'd like him to give to our pressure, all of the training is finished. From there, the repetition is all for ourselves, to convince ourselves that the horse knows what we're asking. Repetition can also create automatic, entrained responses, which is what is often used as proof that an animal, or a person, is effectively trained. It is a totally valid form of communication - this form of communication, though, is less about honoring the partnership and fluid communication and more about becoming dominant over predictable behaviors.

When we can be clear with ourselves in what we're asking, a horse will give to our pressure spontaneously as if we've been repeating the effort for years. All it really takes is clarity, knowing what we are truly asking for with this pressure, free from emotional charge, free from thoughts of punishment, for the person or the horse, if it doesn't happen "the right way."

This dance with Cooper, asking for his left hind foot, is not about training. Going through the conversation with his feet is all about inviting him into a new perspective, giving him the space to see for himself that his foot is no longer being held forcefully. Giving him the space to see for himself that my presence is different than the habitual battle.

The conversation isn't really even about his foot! It's about his breath. His presence. It's about his willingness to stay fluid in his own body rather than go into survival mode, which is how he learned to cope with some of the things people brought to him.

The most effective way to bring a horse out of resistance is not training, it is listening.

Where We're Heading

"What I'd really like is for Cooper to be able to go down the trail comfortably, maybe not by himself, with another horse, but I want to be able to trust him and for him to know that we trust each other." That is a very reasonable request from Lynda, from a human perspective!

Because we "train" horses, we also put an expectation on them that it is their job to trust and be trustworthy, and whatever "trustworthy" means can change in any moment. It can feel like a lot of pressure to a horse in a way that doesn't jive with his or her natural way of being. A horse is wired for communication, which not necessarily trust the way humans would like it to be. In horse-world, if you are surrounded by those who will communicate what they see, what they sense, then trust isn't an issue. It's more like there is a constant stream of updates for the general state of being of a group, and everyone is as aware as they'd like to be. From there, it is each individual's unique connection and response to this communication that recommends the next action.

When we train horses to be something, to act and react in a particular way because we think that will be what keeps us safe, we may actually be undermining their innate ability to look out for our safety by restricting the whole conversation.

All of the grooming conversations and foot handling conversations Cooper and I have been having, as I said, have nothing to do with training. It's all about inviting us both into the same congruent conversation, where we recognize that we are sharing communication with one another, rather than in battle of who's on top. Those battles can change with the wind of our emotions.

It's easy to overlook when we are at battle, to not see it at all. We can be totally convinced that we are creating peace and harmony but actually be in a battle for "good behavior because I said so." We can be at battle with our horse, pushing him to perform as he screams in fear or pain on a sensory level to get our attention, and remain totally convinced that our training methods are effective ones. After all, we are effective at getting the horse to do what we want, right? Isn't that good training?

Inviting a horse out of the battle he's learned as "the way to be with humans" takes listening without an agenda. No agenda for how fast it should go, no agenda for what he should know, no agenda for what comes first or second. No agenda for what it should look like when we're finished. I know that Lynda would like to be riding Cooper out on the trail and feeling safe, and I honor that this is what she wants. But I'm not going to listen to Cooper with the caveat that what he's sharing had better lead to what Lynda wants. I'm not listening with my senses colored by expectation that he should feel safe, that he should even want to go out on the trail. The freedom created from releasing expectations is what allows us to actually move in the direction of going out on the trail in harmony. No agenda does not mean no results. It means, "I'm listening."

My presence communicates that it feels wonderful to know and be with each other. Whatever he brings to the conversation, if it has something to do with trail riding or not, is welcome in my world. Living beings feel the gentleness of that space, the space that does not judge or evaluate their expression, that does not remove love if their way of being does not match mine. And this kind of infinite patience can bring immediate results.

Expanding The Conversation

Cooper let me know he's ready to start riding. How do I know? What did I sense?

One day after we finished grooming and cleaning feet, I felt a totally joyous sense like my heart was being lifted onto his back! Even though we were standing together near some grass, finishing up for the day, I felt so light, like I just wanted to jump up and ride right then and there!

I knew it wasn't a desire from my own mind - I was completely content being with him on the ground. My translation for this sensory communication is that he gave me the invitation to ride with him. Not on him, but with him. "I'm ready for a riding partnership. I have a lot to share with you."

"Thank you so much, my friend!"

There has been tremendous criticism from a portion of the equestrian population that just being with a horse on the ground, just doing groundwork, games and loving interactions is not a valid way to be with horses. Some people have some pretty harsh criticism for others who have no desire to ride. But there are so many people who, when they feel safe enough to tell the truth, will say that when they were small, they didn't really want to ride, they just wanted to be with the horses, to feed them, to groom them, to be with them: "I took riding lessons because that was the only way to be near horses." As time went on, riding was just "the way," and they learned to compete, to strive, to dominate, even though it wasn't in their heart. None of this is bad, it's just one of the ways we are taught to override our heart.

Another whole group of people just want to ride or have the horse do what it's told! They don't have interest in groundwork; the relationship they want is for the horse to do what they ask and not question it. The horses, of course, will give to these people with as much love and honor as those whose feet don't leave the ground.

How can one way of being with horses be better than another? The horses are here to partner with us in whatever way we will allow, whatever way we will show up for them. If that means standing in a pasture and being admired from afar, if it means playing four chukkers of polo a week, if that means pulling wagons, if it means traveling in trailers across a continent to jump obstacles in different cities, if it means lining up to go from freedom in the wild to chutes and corrals, or if it means being photographed for a poster calling for an end to slaughter, horses are available to humanity. We can ask of them whatever we'd like, and the more aware we are of our true motivations, the more the horses will show us their heart and help us see ours in ways we don't even know how to ask for.

When I felt the invitation, I didn't go get the saddle right that minute. Cooper and I walked over to the great grazing area and munched on some food, swimming in this new expansion of our relationship. Rather than jump on and make it happen, I just let the sense of that invitation be our new truth together, in our shared space, his presence connecting with mine. The truth is, neither of us is available for injury. Why would we be? And now we know that he is hearing me and I am hearing him.

The greatest "training" tool we have is our own presence. It's what the horse whisperer gurus are trying to teach. Their magic is their own presence, bringing a horse into what we currently call a submissive state. Maybe they wouldn't use the same vocabulary I use, but when they are with a horse, the "guru-person" is speaking most profoundly with their own presence, no matter what techniques they use, whether they would talk about it that way or not.

What we call dominant and submissive behaviors are so much more than those labels. It's easy to see one horse push another out of the way and say "that's the dominant horse." What is dominance, really? And what about it makes humanity so compelled to emulate it?

In the animal kingdom, life is about the life of the body. Everything that happens beyond the body is not questioned. Science calls it "survival," and teaches that whoever gets the food and water and shelter will survive to reproduce. Science has told us about that in countless ways while studying many species.

But there is a tremendous difference between that form of survival and our own. The difference lies in our ability to change our perspective.

Animals are not of a consciousness that would prompt them to build a truck to make it easier to access the pastures just over the next mountain - they just walk there. They are not of the consciousness that would create chemical compounds called plastics and new materials that catch rainwater without degrading - they walk in a direction they feel and/or know to come to water. Their creativity is different, their survival is different. If we try to go into their world to be "dominant" the way we observe them to be with each other, we are missing so much of the story.

Over millenia, we have convinced ourselves that human survival depends on work, earning, pleasing others, coming up with the next great invention, keeping our spouse happy, providing something of perceived value. These things actually have nothing to do with survival, until we program our belief systems. These things have everything to do with domination.

We dominate markets, we dominate cultures, we dominate each other's belief systems, actions, thoughts, emotions, expression. We dominate our own senses with judgments of what should be. We have used this kind of dominance in response to a sense of survival when, truly, our survival was never in question. This is not the kind of dominance we observe between the animals.

The behavior we observe in animals, the behavior we call "dominant" is far more about stating, "This is who I am" than it is about bodily survival. Of course, we can analyze the situation and track a "dominant" behavior among animals and observe how it will assist the pack or the herd to find more food, more water, more shelter. But animals' behaviors, even in natural situations, are still communicating, "This is who I am in the herd/pack/pride/flock/school. This is my unique contribution." It's not dominance that creates survival in the animal kingdom, it's eating, drinking, sleeping and communing.

When we use dominance in training animals, we are not actually stepping into their world and their language. What we are showing them is, "This is who I am as a human. This is my unique contribution." And the animals will, invariably, respond without judging it. Their response is, "Okay. There you are. Here is how I respond to you."

Trying to use techniques of dominance, which are the foundation of most animal training, may not communicate who we truly are in our hearts. In other words, using these techniques may be communicating an incongruency between who I am and how I behave. Animals see that disconnect from a mile away. Some will go along with it and not call us on it. Some have such a hard time reconciling the discontinuity that they either totally give in, or they totally refuse to participate, which looks like "bad behavior." Most of the time, though, the animals will show us behaviors that we call "bad behaviors" to communicate to us, "Here is what it feels like to be me with you while you are being like that." At this moment, most

people don't realize their opportunity to see themselves --
instead, many go further into dominance.

Being with horses is about knowing ourselves, whether we
want to admit it or not. It's about knowing what we are
bringing to the conversation. The horses will share what they
sense, and they never lie, cheat or judge. The more clearly we
understand ourselves, without judging ourselves, the more
simple and clear the horses become. The freedom, love, beauty,
connection and sheer fun we feel in their presence, that is who
we are.

There has been very little support for being with horses, or
anyone else for that matter, outside of a paradigm of
dominance. But a new paradigm is present. It is a paradigm of
awareness, not only of ourselves, but of a greater truth around
us without the confining need to simply survive. We are
beginning to see beyond a life of carnal survival. Expanding
our awareness of the animal kingdom, in the physical and
energetic worlds of sensory communication shows us how we
can listen without having to overcome anything, participate
without winning or losing, and integrate perspectives that may
be vastly different than our own.

Intention

*Intention is a magnificent tool to begin opening our
awareness and seeing just how powerful we are. We can
intend a certain outcome, to be here, or there, or to be*

anything we can think up. And that is a brilliant beginning to awareness of what is right in front of us!

You see, I AM here! The body would not be functioning if my unique life force were not present. When I place my awareness on what already IS, I amplify the sensation of my own presence through my body. I begin to know that I am here because my body communicates it. This knowing is a tangible sensation that transcends doubt. Being here is not an intention, it is a truth that vibrates as love. The truth of your love is the vibration of your uniqueness, the same thing that people are talking about when they say, "Shine your light for the whole world to see!"

The real question we want to ask is, "Who Am I?"

Which leads to, "What does that look like, and feel like, expressed through this body?"

And then, "How do I know?"

The animals are guides through this little series of queries, because in the animal world, there is no questioning of "Who am I," or "Do I want to be here?" Animals do not have the consciousness to doubt, contemplate or pretend to be anything they are not, including being here. This is probably the greatest sense of why they are so therapeutic for humanity, so healing. Immersing ourselves in their congruent vibration of "here I AM" helps us remember what that feels like.

Intention happens in the mind. What intention really says is, "Okay...I feel safe enough to let this happen now." You see, the mind's job is to keep us safe and predictable - to keep us from walking in front of a moving bus, or to know how to drive a car or balance a checkbook. The mind serves our functionality, but it is not a sensory instrument.

When we are searching to remember and embody the truth of who we are, are we searching for a formula? Or are we searching for a sense? Some people call it peace, some call it joy, some call it bliss, nirvana, zero-point, etc. What we call it really doesn't matter...it is a vibration, the frequency of truth that reveals who we truly are as we walk through our lives. It is our body, not our mind that communicates that sense.

The animals are always living at a frequency that is totally congruent with what is True for them, as who they are. The truth is not something we decide, it is a vibration, a sense that our bodies know innately, that our mind can translate into action.

We are taught, bullied and convinced to make many things more significant than our own heart, but our heart will always find us, always beckon our return. We can begin the journey by intending to be aware of that vibration again, to know that we ARE here, but once we can sense it, intention no longer serves. As we unlearn everything that no longer serves us, we reveal our true presence to interact with the rest of the world. This is why we came here!

Horses are always communicating through their presence, their natural expression. Our own thoughts create filters that can make it difficult to have clarity in what the horses are communicating, and that's okay. Humans have a very different mind structure than horses - not greater than or less than, but different. Humans process information differently, and unlike horses, humans have the capability of judging and deceiving themselves. Self-deception can get in the way of clarity.

The courage to be honest with ourselves, whether it's out loud or silently, is another uniqueness of humanity. Animals don't need that capacity, because they are not capable of deceiving themselves. Our courage to see our own truth is not just a gift to ourselves, but a gift to the horses, the rest of the animal kingdom, the children, and all of humanity as well.

Enchantment

There is an amazing and unique connection between horses and humans, a kind of bond between species that parallels life-partners. Horses are enchanted with humanity. The entire species will show up in service in so many different ways, and all we need do is ask. Humanity is enchanted with horses. We see it in art, myth, literature, music, industry, sport, healing, life and the advancement of our own evolution. In the collective heart of humanity is a connection with horses that knows, without question, that when we ask, the horses will give, an unconditional partnership.

Opening to recognize the unconditional giving from the horses, without judging humanity, can present us with a whole new level of awareness and availability for communion. Maybe we become open to seeing love for horses in other humans, even when those other humans may treat horses very differently than we would. Can we look past the discomfort long enough to recognize the heart? The courage to be honest with ourselves in how we feel and why we do what we do opens our own hearts even more to animals and other people.

Can we honor others who have horses in their lives, knowing that the horses are not judging their own treatment? Can we see each other the way horses see us? Can we see our collective heart that is in love with horses, and meet each other in that place?

Pragmatic Application

A "guru horse whisperer" stands in the middle of a round pen. Someone brings in a wild horse, running, looking for escape. The human stands in the middle of the round pen, just being in the middle. There is a conversation going on in that round pen, one that can be easily overlooked because it is not often articulated into words.

We can watch the scene and say that the person uses body language to communicate leadership. We can watch as that person might push the horse's hips in one direction or another, getting the horse to move their feet and call it dominance, because that is what we've observed in herd behavior. We can watch that person mimic herd behavior in many ways and work the horse into a place of acceptance, asking for what we call "submission." We can observe body language, gestures, sounds, use of the eyes and energetic pressure. We can study the human's behaviors, body language, gestures, and we can go home and mimic the "guru" who mimicked his or her interpretation of the horse. Sometimes we have the same kind of effect, other times, not so much. And there are people who are convinced that they can never do what "horse whisperers" do.

The truth is, everyone is a horse whisperer. Including you! It is already happening all of the time, whether you are aware of it or not! You ARE a horse whisperer. The difference between each of us and how effectively we use our abilities comes down to two things: awareness and absence of judgment.

What is it about the "gurus" that sets them apart from the people who study them? What is the turning point that people reach where they confidently become a "whisperer?" What makes someone available to a horse like that? Is it talent? Training?

Anyone can throw a ball, right? Whether it's a plastic ball or a baseball, everyone with a hand can hold a ball in their hand and propel it in one direction or another.

Not everyone, though, can throw a baseball at 98 miles per hour and hit a target the size of a dinner plate. What is the difference?

The person who can throw a ball 98 miles per hour has a totally different awareness of their ability, of their body, of the ball, the game, the vision, the space and how it all fits together. Whether they are able to describe their awareness or not, it's there, and it's what we call "talent."

In the same light, everyone can communicate with animals. Some people have awareness that parallels a 98 mph fastball pitcher, with incredible ability and agility, whether they know how to talk about it or not. Others are communicating with great mastery but no particular awareness that their ability is even an actual "ability."

The people who don't have the same awareness are still receiving communication from the animals, from the horses, but the way they identify with it may be totally different.

We are always "whispering." The way to expand our awareness, to expand our ability and step into further clarity and understanding is to start noticing where the communication is already happening. Cooper assists this awareness by communicating, "Here's how it feels to be me with you when you show up like that."

With something that can seem as intangible as communicating with animals, it helps to be able to see the communication that already exists. For example, if I ask my dog to sit, how am I asking? What does it feel like when he responds with a sit? What image is in my mind as I ask? How does it feel if I ask and he doesn't sit? What emotions, images and senses come if he doesn't sit when I ask?

These questions and others along the same lines begin to open our perspective to new awareness. It takes courage to ask. The courage is to notice what we are feeling, even though we might be judgmental of our own state of being. When we can let the answers come without immediately judging ourselves wrong, or supremely right, we're well on our way!

It also helps to open our perspective to communication as a sensory exchange. People will say that you can't teach feel, and maybe that's right -- maybe feel isn't something you teach, it's something you notice and acknowledge because it's already there. Of course it's something you're born with...you're human! It's impossible to be at a "wrong" level of awareness or ability. You are in the perfect spot to expand what you know, what you sense.

Judgment can muddy the waters when we find ourselves with thoughts like, "I should be seeing pictures, right?" or, "I haven't studied enough, so I won't get it." Or even, "It's not going to happen with this horse … there is no connection here."

One of the strongest barriers to expanding our awareness sounds like, "Oh yes, I know that. I've been doing that for years." Judgments can show up as "negative" or "positive." At either end of the spectrum, they are creating limiting barriers for our awareness.

Judgments are not truths, they are opinions. They create obstacles for communication to dance around in order to be seen. Judgment affects everything in life in this same way.

If we can show up without judgment of how the communication should be happening, the horses will find ways to reach us! Cooper currently communicates his sense of connection through biting with a sense of invasion -- the judgment that his expression is "bad" leads to domination of his behavior. Without judgment, his behavior simply communicates his sense of the current interaction and his willingness to step into a different interaction.

When a teacher or trainer says to you, "Watch what I do ..." you might play a game with yourself. Instead of watching what they do, watch what they feel. Sense what they feel. You have that capability. It is so naturally part of who you are. It is the sensory connection that brings us together with animals, into camaraderie and communion with each other.

It can take courage, because opening up to feel and sense brings us directly into awareness of parts of ourselves we may have been hiding, or hiding from. But opening in this way in the company of horses, who are never judging us, can be one of the safest, most amazing journeys we ever take in our lives, whether we ever sit in a saddle or not.

Dissolving The Past

So Cooper has invited me to ride. There is so much more to riding than just expecting the horse to do what we ask. And at the same time, there is such simplicity that it takes almost nothing at all.

I have no particular goal or agenda with Cooper, other than to be his friend. Of course, there is the request that he be a trustworthy trail horse, that he stop the mouth games, that he let go of throwing his hips and shoulders into people, that he not run away, etc. As he is given the opportunity to see a human of a different perspective, he becomes available for a different kind of friendship with people. Whether or not he ever gets out on the trail as the "right" kind of trustworthy horse per request, well, he'll let us know how far he wants to go in that direction, and with whom. But it would totally defeat the purpose of creating a safe trail horse for me to "re-train" him through force.

Cooper's invitation to step forward into riding, into the next facet of our relationship, feels like an honor. Riding is not something I am drawn to naturally. Without the invitation directly from the horse, riding feels to me like total domination. With the invitation, though, in communion, riding is one of the most intimate interactions of communion available to me.

Cooper is around 10 years old, and he's ridden with several other people. With some riders he will offer light, beautiful movements; and with others he will offer to buck them off. As he and I go forward together, the biggest contribution I can make to our relaxed and wonderful time together is to set aside all of the stories and the events he's experienced in his past. Why would I want to recreate any of that when I have a pristine opportunity to create a brand new connection, a brand new conversation that goes beyond anxiety, battle and resistance?

People will tell me stories about what a horse has been through, stories that are "good" and stories that are "bad." If I were to listen to those as if they describe the horse in front of me, I'd be immediately at a disadvantage. The tales are largely stories of the misunderstanding and misinterpretations of people, of their judgments and fears of their own ability or inability to be in control, to perform, to create a certain outcome. Those stories don't describe the horse who is standing in front of me. Those stories don't describe my presence and communication.

Cooper and I went to the round pen together. My presence still communicates that I am unavailable to be injured. I carry no expectation that he would behave in a way that would injure me. I know that I am free to remove myself with a "no thank you" should my senses communicate danger.

I ask him to walk forward during my conversation with him, and he can let me know he hears me by walking forward. I offer him no reason to not walk forward, for example, the fear that if he doesn't walk fast enough, it won't be good enough. I don't care how fast he walks. I don't care how slow he walks. That he walks forward simply because I ask is a gift!

There is a facet of conventional training that says you need to make a horse march forward, that you should want the horse to use a lot of energy to prove that she or he is responsive and willing to work. According to that method of training, Cooper and I would be big fat failures. As Cooper walks forward, he is dragging himself. I wouldn't even call his walk slow, I'd call it sticky. And it comes with a total resistance, as he looks outside the roundpen, and his shoulder, the one closest to me, feels like a shield that's twice it's actual size.

I could use a whip and emotional force to "get the horse to move forward" faster, stronger, on purpose. But what would that serve, other than to create another battle of dominance and submission? I'm not after a battle, in fact, I'm being a new perspective, a new way of being. Forcing him forward does not feel new. It doesn't feel like Me. It feels like domination.

I ask him to walk forward, and he moves his feet. "Thank you so much, my friend! I love your walk!"

And his eye watches me, walking his sticky walk, sharing his story with me. He's prepared to be forced, he's prepared to resist. He's prepared to explode, rebel, resist force with force … it's what he's been taught by the training system that expects that a horse "should" have a strong forward walk. It isn't the trainer-people that create the sticky walk and readiness to explode, it's the training-expectations that a horse should be something other than he is. The battle is in the expectation that we must force a horse to give to us rather than creating the space for the horse to give us, more than we ever could have asked for.

"Thank you so much! I love your walk!" is the conversation in my whole body. It is true for me! My presence vibrates it.

He watches me with a wary eye. He looks outside the round pen. He shows me a "cold shoulder," and his steps move forward at a snail's pace, about 2 feet with every stride. How could I possibly take it personally?

"I love you! Thank you so much."

He uses his energy to push into me, to push back, not against me, but against his past experience of being forced forward. I want to be very clear with you … he is not resisting me, he is resisting his experience. It's not personal. I am a whole new conversation, a whole new perspective. Sometimes it just takes a bit of movement, at any pace, to recognize it.

My request is that he continue moving forward once around the round pen without stopping. I support his forward movement, mostly through my total enjoyment that it's even happening! A few times he offers to stop walking, and he looks at me. My body is light, and it moves in a way that supports his continuing forward walk. Maybe my arm comes up a bit, my shoulders open in the direction he's going. My voice and my energy, my space, all say, "Wow! How awesome it is that you are walking forward!" Imagine how different that feels than becoming predatory, cracking a whip, acting as if severe punishment is on its way.

I know that in my heart the most important and valuable part of this interaction is the congruent communication - it's what I want, it's what he wants. What it looks like or how fast it happens really isn't my business. My business is to be the new perspective, the new conversation for both of us.

Once around, and I ask him to whoa. I ask gently by transferring my energy and space out ahead of him, as if I'm simply closing a gate 12 feet ahead. Here he shows me a different flavor of resistance and begins to walk forward faster rather than respond to my request! Brilliance! He has been so creative in learning how to play with humans, to keep the interactions going rather than simply submit to training. After all, if we just submit and do what we're told, the game ends, right?

I let him play his game, and I let him win. He is right - he doesn't have to stop walking just because I asked. He doesn't have to stop just because I can communicate through energy or use the tool of the round pen. He is totally capable of plowing right over me, doing whatever he wants. So, I re-tune my conversation and, rather than being a force to make him stop walking, I become a presence where horses stop walking. It's what "whoa" feels like. And he stops walking.

"Thank you so much!" And his eyes are bright, curious. I walk to his shoulder as his head drops. There are no face games, no mouth coming at me. And he's breathing. "Thank you, my friend."

People are taught that people need to be taught how to be with horses, to communicate. Our minds are conditioned to think that unless we learn something from someone who has a certification, or seems to have more of some kind of experience than we have, then we are somehow lacking the ability we need to play, live and be with horses. The truth is, it's just not true!

Each of us is born with the capacity to listen, to feel, to sense and to respond to our senses with wisdom. When we receive facilitation from others, our abilities can expand that much faster. But even without deliberate facilitation, our innate nature is to expand, and awareness happens whether we seek it or not, unless we deliberately remain confined.

If it is our desire to perform and be judged, then there absolutely IS a right way that will satisfy the judgment. There are countless ways, modalities and disciplines that will teach a proper way to be with horses. The paradigm of training and performance has installed the illusion that there is a "right" way to be with horses, even though 9 out of 10 experts will disagree.

It can be valuable to explore whether we are wanting to be with horses because we are in love with horses, or if we are using horses to carry us to a place where we approve of ourselves. Neither is the right way to be or the wrong way to be. But when we have clarity in the answer to that question, the horses are able to give us so much more. And we are open to receive their efforts without resistance.

Cooper gets a shoulder rub for a few moments, and then I ask him to change directions and walk once around the other way. I tell him what I'm going to ask of him, in words, "Okay, I'd like you to walk the other direction, too, just because it feels good. Thank you!" And I guide his movement with my body, my energy, my awareness. I make it part of my own truth that Cooper walks forward in the other direction, and he feels this.

In "training" a horse, the convention would be that you have to make the horse go an equal time or distance in both directions. In communication with a horse, you ask for something, in this case a walk, with a sense of how it feels when we know the connection is present. It doesn't matter how many steps it takes and in which direction.

I ask the horse to participate with me, as opposed to perform for me. Acknowledging the sense of a horse being "with" me is exponentially more clear than a simple release of pressure. And the acknowledgement can be the release of my breath, knowing that this breath is an integral part of the conversation.

In his heart, and in relationship to humans, Cooper is wanting connection, not dominance. As I let my presence be what is true for me, I give him the invitation to connect with me. The same way he extended an invitation for me to ride, I extend an invitation to connect.

The pictures in my mind of him walking, the way I raise my hand, the way I open my right shoulder to suggest that there is open space in that direction ... all of that is secondary to what I ask through my senses and my heart, "Please walk in this direction."

"Please walk forward to the right, Cooper. Thank you." I ask him for forward without force, "... and your speed is up to you. Thank you." I am congruent through my mind, my body, my heart, my energy. With this sort of an invitation, walking forward can feel light, easy, full of gratitude. It's the same feeling as when everything just goes perfectly even though we weren't even trying!

His natural speed at the walk is a bit faster and much more fluid than what he's offering me right now. That is so okay with me! This is not about making the horse perform. It is about inviting and acknowledging a sense of camaraderie and mutual understanding. Once we share that sense, we can ask each other for anything knowing that we are on the same page. Whether we're in a round pen or on a trail, we both want the same thing, which is whatever keeps that connection intact.

He walks to the right. Before he does, though, he scans me with his eye and his senses. He feels for any incongruency, opportunity or invitation to battle me. He feels for whether or not I'm going to battle him. In other words, he looks to see if I am feeling defensive or offensive. He finds none of that, and his familiar pattern of battling me simply dissolves. He walks forward to the right, in 2 foot strides, watching and waiting for a forceful message from me that never comes.

"Thank you, Sir. Thank you." And it's time to go eat grass.

You see, my goal is not to train this horse to run in circles in a round pen or to callous himself to his own anxiety in order to carry a human out on the trail. My goal, which is more like a way of being, is to not be dominant or submissive.

If I were to reproduce what other people have learned and taught about softening a horse using the tools of a round pen with pressure and reward, what am I really doing there? Am I partnering with a horse? Or am I forcing the horse into a survival state so that I can present myself as the savior?

I could use the mindset of predator and prey, invoking the horse's natural response to threat and get him to perform at my request. But that is not what I am about. I am not interested in breaking a horse down into his instinctive survival mode in order to get his attention and submission. There is so much more available to us in communication and partnership with horses as equals rather than animals we are destined to conquer.

We will always have the option to conquer, although we may find it less and less appealing once the sense of communion, of communication makes itself clear.

Accessible To Everyone

I have a lifetime of being with horses, facilitating, healing, teaching, and training. This is true. Some people use this as an argument to say they can't do what I do. It's understandable to believe that we need to be performing and practicing something for years before we master it, before we are "good" at it. That way of thinking about our abilities has been taught, and therefore accepted as true for a long time. That perspective, though, can easily become a barrier to the real truth.

We all have natural abilities to communicate with all of life, and in fact we do communicate with all of life, all of the time! Everyone is welcome to declare that they can't, that they don't have the ability to sense and listen on these levels. That declaration does not mean the ability is inaccessible, though. What you can't yet see in yourself, perhaps you will allow others to see in you, to assist you by seeing it for you, and guide your awareness back to it.

The animals in our lives can assist us to see and become more of our own true self, our own true nature, when we are open to that perspective. The interactions between us can be evolutionary every day. Animals are just as enamored with us as we are with them, and sometimes it takes a little recalibration in our own perspective to be able to sense that.

We are sharing the planet, evolving side-by-side with them, assisting each other.

Freeing a horse from a way of being that isn't who he truly is has many facets to it. It can seem really complex, and at the same time, it's very simple.

Repetition is not necessarily the most effective tool, for the horse or the person. The foundation of all safe travels together, whether it is on the trail, or just between the round pen and paddock begins by honoring the communication. He recognizes that I asked for something, and I recognize that he gave as much as he had to give. Holding hands with my friend, we create a dance that lets us both dissolve the past and become a new perspective.

Horses feel the space created by this perspective. They feel the kindness, the harmony of it. They feel when we step away from being a predator, away from domination, and they respond differently to us. When they do, we have the opportunity to open up to a whole different way of being. We've been forcing horses into a false sense of fight-or-flight survival in order to "train" them for thousands of years, and it has worked very well to get horses to do what we tell them to do. We are in a different time, though, when more and more people are feeling in their hearts, knowing in their knowing that there is a different way.

Stepping into a different way means that it will feel different than the old, familiar way. It will look different. The timing may be different. The goals, the outcomes, the expectations may all be different. And the unfamiliarity may be uncomfortable at first.

I've worked with trainers who feel the difference in their bodies immediately when they step out of a context of dominance. They sense the difference in their horses, and it can feel like being a beginner again.

I remind them that they don't have to buy into this perspective. There is no rule that says this is the "New Right Way To Be." There are no rules! I tell people, "Please, if it is too strange, too loose for you, please just do what you know -- there is nothing wrong with how you do what you do!"

The consistent response is, "NO! I don't want to go back, this feels so much better ... but it really feels different!" Sometimes the trainers feel a little insecure, because the expansion into a new perspective can feel like you're starting over again, a beginner again. It's not about starting over at all. It is an expansion of what you already do that will integrate more of who you truly are. It is opening to a much bigger awareness that expands harmony simply through acknowledgement of the harmony that is already there. This level of awareness does not require repetition to train a horse. The awareness itself creates consistency.

There Is A Difference

There is a difference between repetition and consistency. Repetition is doing the same thing over and over again, expecting and engendering the same response. Consistency doesn't need to see a precisely repeated response to know that it has accomplished what it set out to do.

I could take Cooper into the round pen and do the same exercise each day. In doing so, my hopes would be that he interprets my actions the way I want him to. There would likely be some resistance in there, some misunderstanding, but hopefully, as long as I repeat the same motions, the same exercises, and the same relative timing, he and I would eventually fall into a pattern of responses that has been built on these repetitive actions. This is training.

The concept of repetition doesn't really take into account the state of being of either the human or the horse. Simply repeating body movements, sounds, exercises, expectations is not necessarily the same as communicating a consistent message to a horse.

Consider if one day we show up to do our exercises and we're feeling great. We've just had lunch with a good friend, we've spent the past hour laughing, our thoughts are on good memories and good food. We go through our exercises with our horse almost without thinking, and our horse responds well to our exercises. We feel open and fluid and decide it was a "good" day.

The next day, we have a morning full of phone calls demanding things of us we don't want to give. We spend the first part of the day feeling attacked and invaded. We show up at the barn feeling like there is no way out and we don't know what to do next, but it's time to work our horse in the repetitive exercises to reinforce our training. We do our best to hide our state of mind from our horse so we can get our exercises done. The horse shows us anxiety today, resistance, spookiness. We may feel frustration with our horse because yesterday everything was fine. Yesterday our training seemed to be going well. We begin to identify problems in our horse, something to correct so that our horse is better again tomorrow.

It's easy in these scenarios to try to fix the horse when the horse is just being the horse in response to us. A more gentle way to move through this natural fluctuation of human thought and emotion is to listen to our own state of mind, to feel our own emotional state and our body. If I'm willing to acknowledge that my own body is tense, even on subtle levels, because of my own outside world, the horse will have the space and freedom to give to me despite the tension. If I'm trying to fake it, trying to pretend I don't feel the way I feel, to a horse, that feels like a battle...because that's exactly what it is. We're trying to "train" our horse to give without resistance while we live in a state of resistance within ourselves.

This is the difference between training and communicating, or simply listening. Training a horse makes great assumptions about who a horse is, and how she or he will respond, as if all horses will always respond the way we expect horses to respond, based in our observations of a fight or flight consciousness.

I know it can sound strange at first, but not all horses are most comfortable responding to people in what we consider to be normal herd behavior. A few years ago I was asked to meet with a horse and the woman who had been working with him. He was a big bay gelding, and the story went that he wanted always to be on top of people. Hand walking could be precarious because he wanted to be touching the people all of the time -- not in a malicious way, but he wanted to be touching shoulders at least. Trying to "train" him out of it only caused more anxiety for him, for other horses and for people.

Lunging this horse was nearly impossible. He just wouldn't stay out on the line. He'd come in on the circle no matter how strong the suggestion that he stay out. And his anxiety would escalate to the point where he felt dissociated and totally disconnected.

So when I sat with him and listened to both the person and the horse, I wasn't looking for remedies, I wasn't looking for problems. I was looking for how it felt to be in this interaction between them. I wanted clarity on a sensory level first and foremost to understand this horse's world-view. This trainer is very successful in working with horses, producing horses who are very happy competing in shows with confidence. To not be able to reach this horse was truly a puzzle for her.

As I listened, I connected with this unique horse as a horse, but I did not limit my perception to what I know horses to be ... or what I think I know horses to be. My perspective opened wide up so that I would be available to any concept, image or sensory communication that could possibly come through. The trainer asked me what she can do differently to be able to reach this horse, to create a fulfilling life for him as well as his riders and handlers.

The people were working this horse and communicating with him as if he sees the world just like every other horse. After all, he is a thoroughbred, a gelding, 8 years old, never on the track, years of training in the hunter/jumper world -- we should be able to work with him based on that information, right? But it was obvious he wasn't seeing the world the way we would expect a horse with that story to respond. He was listening energetically, telepathically, and at the same time, looking for guidance and clues for where to go next through physical touch. He was looking for communication on levels and dimensions beyond our normal understanding of how a horse sees the world.

He wanted a sense of those around that his body could respond to, and that response would be so consistent with his sense of safety that there is no dissonance in his body. He didn't use his visual sense like other horses; he was looking for connection and communication on other levels. The best image to offer to describe his world was as if he were a fish who is looking for a school.

What felt really natural to him was to be in what I would call a collective consciousness, where there are many individuals moving as one. A herd is like that, to be sure, but this horse had a very strong sense of the possibility of a tight, collective unit that he found himself lacking. He wasn't able to feel the energetic connection that his senses had him "looking" for, so he used his body to create contact and feel connected to something outside of himself. That something outside himself turned out to be a human body. Of course he wasn't comfortable lunging -- there was no way for him to feel connected so far away from his "school," especially when the closest member was standing relatively still.

Being in a horse-show environment, he was housed in a stall by himself, so he had no physical contact with other horses. When it came time to be out and in motion, he was being ridden, or turned out in a paddock by himself. He wanted his sense of awareness and direction in his body to be a very, very rich exchange of multi-dimensional senses. This is what he was available for, and he was doing everything he could to invite someone else into his world.

As I listened to him, I described his world to the trainer as if he were more connected with schooling-fish consciousness than horse consciousness, at least as he relates to others. Some may interpret that he was a fish in a previous lifetime, and they wouldn't be wrong. But the question of the moment was, "What can we do differently to be able to ride and show this horse without having him physically on top of us all of the time." So, we let the information come in a way that is relevant to the moment.

As I explained his state of mind and heart to his trainer, I shared techniques she can use to open herself up energetically to be available in the ways that will make herself obvious to him. Becoming aware of her own thoughts, of her energy, and beginning to use her natural ability to expand her presence built the foundation for a new way to communicate with this horse. First and foremost, though, she would need to acknowledge that he was operating differently than what we learned to expect of horses. She's being invited to expand her awareness of what a horse "is."

I asked if she would be open to letting him feel like a fish in a school, to letting herself feel like a fish in a school, and together they move forward through their environment, never out of contact because there is a shared energetic field between them. She was willing to go there.

Opening to a different perspective like this can change a horse's entire way of being immediately. It comes down to dropping our judgment of what a horse, or any individual "should" be, or how they "should" be responding to us, blowing the doors wide open to sense how they actually ARE responding to us. It is such a gift to give that space to any horse, or any living creature. When we release our stranglehold on what we expect to see, miracles happen.

I offered her suggestions on how to restructure her conversation with him so that it would be more relevant in his world, so he would sense and know that she is seeing him, feeling him. With a big open heart, she stepped into a new way of being with him, and he responded immediately. It wasn't a matter of training, it was a matter of listening, not only to the horse, but to what we bring to the conversation as well. She and the fish-horse had great shifts together and their entire world opened up.

When we use training techniques that are sold to us as an approach that works for all horses, something that is considered a derivative of the horses' natural behavior, we are actually making a big assumption about horses' natural behavior. These training techniques are expecting horses to behave the way we observe horses to behave. My question is, where are the edges of our awareness? What are we truly available to see in our observations?

When a horse doesn't respond with the survival behaviors we expect, it is assumed that the techniques we tried just "don't work." And when natural training techniques just aren't working, more often than not, the blame is put on the horse for not understanding, or actually being "untrainable." It's not the horses' fault.

There is no fault on the human's part, either. Please don't misunderstand my statement. It's not the horse's fault, it's not the human's fault, it's not the technique's fault. If we want to assign fault, let's make it judgment's fault -- the judgment that every horse should fit within the structure of my expectation.

It's just a total misunderstanding. And lucky for us, there is always a way to change our understanding!

That is the beauty of being human -- we have the ability to change our perspective, to realize a new way of being, and to let that transition happen. The animals evolve as well, come to new understanding, expand into new versions of themselves right beside us. But they are not the ones prompting the evolution. We are, as we open to a new perspective. The animals walk right next to us, facilitating as they show up and offer, always, "As you wish."

Integrating The Difference

Cooper is already trained. He already knows how to work with people, how to actually work people, through their emotions, their fears, their doubts. This is the training he received when people first started handling him. From that point forward, he has been doing everything he can, in alignment with his own playful heart, to get people to see how to be with a horse without fighting.

His method is to apply enough pressure in the places that really trigger human emotion, the places where we will resort to dominance and force. It's up to the people at that point to recognize their opportunity to dominate or choose a different perspective. The option to go to a new perspective is not widely supported yet. But it is always available.

He's happy to give in whichever direction we lead. The message is the same, "Let's play!" Will we judge that his play is bad? Or wrong? Or can we see it for the communication it is, and dance with him?

The biggest obstruction to the dance is the assumption that his behavior is in any way a personal statement about myself, my ability, my vision, my history or my desires.

When I ask him to walk out to the left in the round pen, he says, "Make me." He gives me a very stiff shoulder and neck, and his feet are anchored into the ground. I could take this personally, as if he is challenging me. I could respond by building up my energy, getting bigger, louder, more threatening. I could take it personally as a challenge to my ability to make a horse go. I could become predatory and aggressive, use my whip on the ground, in the air, or on him. I could start to prove my own ability and do whatever it takes to make the horse go. And he will respond to me accordingly, if I want to go that way.

But I don't. I don't want to get predatory with him, I am a different perspective. I don't want to force him into reacting from instinct. There is a different perspective. There is nothing to prove, no battle to win. And I realize, his behavior has nothing to do with me, my ability, who I am, where I've been or where I'm going. His behavior is just his behavior.

He kicks in with his masterful use of energy to push me just a bit further. I feel it in my heart and my solar plexus, and it is uncomfortable. This is the discomfort he senses when forced to walk in circles for an unclear purpose. He feels pushed, he pushes back.

Many people in this kind of a situation would harden themselves, take it as a challenge, and overcome the behavior with dominance or aggression in one form or another. How much is that the way "training" is taught? But that just seems like a lot of work that neither of us wants to do to prove a pointless point. Why would I need to be a predator to this horse? I'd rather honor his awareness, his brilliance, his state of being, and be his friend.

So, I walked over to him with the halter and lead rope. I rub his shoulder and neck, give him a hug and open my own energy differently. I shift my own presence to dissolve the sense of challenge. I can still feel a bit of that expectation of challenge, as he also has expectations of how humans will behave with him. After all, the round pen is often used as a tool of work and punishment, however well-intended the training might be.

I put the lead rope around his neck, holding it lightly so it will just fall off of him as I let go of it. I ask him again to walk forward to the left in the round pen, suggesting with the lead rope which direction to step, and asking him forward as I stand by his hip. I ask him as if I know nothing of his history, even the history of the past ten minutes. This moment is very different than his past experience, and he steps forward with a very open, innocent eye. I let the lead rope drop from his neck, and together we walk a few steps along the round pen fence. It feels great, open, gentle … and the innocence lasts about five steps. I feel the tension start to build -- whether it was my expectation or his for how long this would last doesn't matter. The building tension communicated that it was time to peel off, give him some space, and shift into something else.

I could have pushed and insisted that he continue to walk because I said so. I could have gone and done that exercise again...over and over, until he responds predictably each time I ask him to walk ahead to the left. But I'm not here to train him. I'm not interested in repetitive responses. I am interested in knowing that he hears me, him knowing that I hear him. I am interested in communication.

As we move closer to riding, to going out on the trail, whether he can do repetitive exercises is far less valuable to our relationship than knowing we can trust each other to listen, even when it's uncomfortable. Repetition of exercises alone won't get that done. Consistency in presence will.

There are those days when the behavior that shows up makes me revisit what I'm doing with Cooper. I often have this feeling that if anyone calling themselves a trainer were watching me, they'd tell me I don't know what the hell I'm doing. It's sometimes hard to tell in those moments if my self-doubt is warranted or not. And those are the moments when I am so grateful that I'm standing next to a horse -- the moment I pause long enough to look at the battle in my own head is the same moment a horse will look at me, straight at me, and acknowledge, "You don't have to be doing that."

When Cooper, or any horse or dog or other being, seems to be fighting with me, challenging me, is it truly the horse challenging me? Or is the horse showing me what it looks like to be the innocent one caught up in the challenge I've given myself? What would it look like if I had nothing to prove, if I took nothing about him personally? What if his behavior was not a statement about me, but was instead an expression of how it feels to be him, given the life he's led up to this point?

And if I surf that perspective, how do I incorporate it into handling and riding with him? How do I incorporate it into my presence?

He still shows me a stiff neck and shoulder. He still throws out that offensively defensive energy that lets me know he can penetrate human emotions if he wants to. He does this as he stands still, watching me with his left eye, waiting to see what I'll bring to him next. And in response, I let out my breath and walk away.

The consistency I want to bring to him is my neutrality about the battle. My consistency is in bringing no offense to him, and no defense against him. Sometimes this means defying all that has been taught about how to train a horse and just walking away from everything we've done up to this point. He's wearing a saddle ... that will have to come off. We're in a round pen ... that will change eventually. The halter is outside the round pen, rather than on him ... that will have to change. So my next dance with him is to take off the saddle, get the halter, and leave the round pen together. I'd like these things to happen with Cooper and me in the same conversation together, as friends who, if we have any kind of goal, have the same goal in mind ... connection.

When he showed me his resistance, when he showed me his invasive, defensive energy, I could have pushed through it and won the argument through force, so to speak. I have all of the skills and tools to "round pen" a horse, to send a horse off to the perimeter of the round pen and cause them to work until I invite them in; I have all of the capability to do this, over and over and over again, hoping the horse realizes that standing next to me, giving me what I ask for, is the lesser evil. But doesn't that mean that, in one respect, I am being an "evil" in his world? Is that who I truly am?

Or, if I'd like to be something different in his world, and my own, I can simply not engage the fight.

The round pen and other tools are often used from the perspective of making a horse work until he figures out what we want. Often, these tools are used when a horse is being difficult, resistant, or we see that she or he is somehow battling us. When we put a horse in a situation to submit, we are actually bringing the battle to him, and it is a battle where he is set up to lose. His only option is to submit because we have overpoweringly dominant tools. Ultimately, no horse wants a fight, especially not with a human. They are here to complement us, to assist us, to share and enjoy life with us. And when we bring this battle to them, we are communicating that we are looking for a battle, even if that battle is intended to lead to harmony. Most will easily submit because the concept of fighting for harmony is so far outside of their natural way of being.

There are those who don't easily submit, though. There are those horses who keep fighting, some who go numb, who turn to anxiety, who injure themselves because this is their natural response to being faced with a battle where there is no way out. Most of the time, these horses are labeled stupid, rank, difficult, dangerous, or untrainable. The truth is, the way they are built as a unique individual within the horse species is simply not compatible with unforgiving dominance.

Equine Redemption, Dufresne's Story

A friend of mine was looking to buy a horse that could be a backyard buddy, a friend to their current quarter horse mare and new member of the family. She didn't want to spend a lot of money, so I suggested we go to the local monthly horse auction to see if we might rescue one of the horses from a potential death sentence. For those of you who are unfamiliar with horse auctions, many times the meat buyers end up taking the unwanted animals at low prices. There are always horses there who have plenty of life left and just need someone to show up and recognize their value, see their heart, and offer them a space where they can just be a loved horse.

We found a few older horses who seemed to be dumped at the auction but still had life left and love to give. My friend decided to bid on two of them.

As the auction proceeded, the horses she liked both went to good homes at good prices! In fact, on that day most of the horses went to good homes! It was refreshing, actually.

Toward the end, the wranglers herded two young bay Arab/Arab-cross stud colts into the ring. It was clear they hadn't been handled and were not in good shape. I didn't see them out in the paddocks before the auction - I think they were brought in at the last second to avoid the scrutiny of potential buyers. They ran around the auction pen, scared and defensive. Nobody raised their arm to place a bid before they were run back out of the auction house. Too small to interest the meat buyers, I believe they went to the Mexican rodeo.

The following month my friend and I went back to the auction yard with high hopes. Again, she found one or two horses that peaked her interest, so we found our seats and waited for the bidding to begin.

The auction went by much like the previous month. The horses she liked went for prices higher than she wanted to pay and found good homes.

And again, just like the previous month, at the very end of the auction, the wranglers herded in one young bay Arab/Arab-cross who was too small to interest the meat buyers. I immediately recognized him as the smaller of the two we saw at the end of last month's auction. He was frantic, traumatized, terrified and was clearly in pain.

The auctioneer launched the bidding at $500, and I heard people chuckle under their breath as if to say, "Yeah...not for THAT thing..."

The price came down, and down as buyers watched this lonely horse search for some escape. $300...$200...$100... I felt a mixture of disgust and anger that these people were so incapable of seeing the beauty and will to live in this horse. I saw it, I knew I could help him, but I wasn't there to buy a horse.

Finally, the auctioneer slowed down and said, "Okay folks, who will take this guy home for $50?"

...ME, apparently! Suddenly I felt my arm shoot up into the air, declaring to
the entire crowd that my heart is the softest.

BANG! The gavel came down, and I now owned a 2 year old Arab-cross who had just been gelded, had no training and a terrible start in life. It's a good thing my friend brought her horse trailer!

Like I said, I did not go to the auction looking to buy a horse. At that point in my life I didn't know if I would have a home for the next month, and my marriage was going poorly at best. But in this particular moment, nothing was more important than helping set this horse on a new path in life.

I paid my $50 in the auction office, plus tax, and bought a $7 plastic halter. The clerks in the office looked at me a little funny and said, "Oh, YOU'RE the one who bought that colt. You'd better be careful. He's out to kill someone."

I wasn't worried.

Out in the paddock yard people collected their horses, either the ones they bought or the ones they didn't sell. I saw my new horse alone in a large paddock. I walked over to the gate and stood there for a while. I just stood there, watching him, letting him watch me, smell me, feel me.

One of the cowboys walked by, playing with his rope, and said to me, "You know, that colt is dangerous. He's out to kill somebody. You won't be able to catch him...it took SIX of us to get him in the trailer last time. You let me know, and I'll come rope him for you when you're ready."

"Okay. Thank you." I replied, and he walked away.

I stayed quiet at the gate and started looking at what kind of condition this boy was really in. He had patches of bare skin where he had fallen or his hair had been whipped away. He had scars where his mouth had been tied shut with a wire. His legs were covered with cuts and sores, and I was surprised when I noticed that he had one white sock - it was hard to see through the caked dirt and dried blood from a wound slightly higher on his leg. All of these wounds were evidence to me that he had been at the Mexican rodeo where horses are whipped into a frenzy so they'll run blindly, then the men display their skill by roping the frantic horse's front legs, bringing them crashing to the ground.

His eyes were still strong and bright, though. He was very aware and alive. His spirit was so strong, totally committed to resisting any attempt to force him into servitude. I was in love with him already!

My sense is that this colt refused to run. My sense is that he chose to stand and be whipped rather than play along with the tripping, and it landed him back at the auction. He had been through so much, seen so much confusion and pain, and he still emanated the will to not only live, but live free of domination and servitude.

I didn't want to own this horse, I didn't want to train him. I wanted to be his friend.

We stood quietly together on opposite sides of the fence for about 15 minutes. I watched him as he discreetly watched me, keeping my own mind clear, my heart open to give him the best chance to assess for himself who I truly am, what I'm about and whether I was here to fight him or to help him.

I opened the gate and stepped into the paddock as if I belonged there, knowing I belonged there. His body faced away from me, and I stayed at least 20 feet away from him. His left ear followed me until I stopped moving my feet. When I did, he turned his head to get a square look at me.

With the plastic halter hanging from my shoulder, I opened myself further and said "Hello" silently. I did not approach him. I did not reach out to him with my hand. I stood still, breathing, sharing with him my sense of relief that he had truly found escape from that life of torture.

He let out a big breath and refocused on me, scanning me more deeply, and as he did, I took a half step back, letting him know that I understand, that I intend no threat. After another five minutes of silent stillness, I turned away and left the paddock.

The auction yard wranglers were watching from behind the fences and around the corners. They KNEW I was crazy. They KNEW I'd never be able to catch this rogue, that I'd never be able to handle him. After all, it took six of them to move him!

I took a break, walked away for ten minutes or so, and talked with my friend about bringing the trailer around. She backed her four horse stock trailer up to a wide chute area, and the guys planted themselves up on the fences to watch the show.

"You're gonna need a rope!" they assured me.

"Okay...thanks." was all I said.

I was quite happy for their attention, though. Call it pride or my own sense of competition, but I wanted them to see what kindness, communication and acceptance can accomplish.

I went back to the paddock and walked directly in. I stepped within about ten feet of him and showed him the halter. He turned his head again to watch me, his feet stock still.

Silently, I communicated to him, "I'd like you to wear this halter and follow me up through this barn to a large trailer where there is hay and soft bedding. I want to take you where you can eat grass and rest with no whips and no ropes."

He felt my offer, contemplated it for a moment and let out a deep sigh. His eyes softened, although not in submission, and he lowered his head in gesture of his invitation to the next step.

I walked straight up to him and gently fit the halter around his head. He stood still, exhaled and licked his lips. I turned myself toward the gate as if he and I had already done this walk hundreds of times together. With the slightest pressure on the halter, I asked him to come with me. The gentle release when he responded communicated to him that trapping him was not my intent. He walked beside me, out the gate and up the breezeway of the auction lot holding pens.

And the wranglers watched in silence.

This young horse, my new hero, felt a bit claustrophobic as we walked past the holding pens, surrounded by gates and fences, shadows and metallic sounds, but he chose to trust me and walk with me. When we made it to the other end of the paddock area, where the trailer was waiting, we had an audience. But this horse and I were focused on each other. I was focused on bringing him safely, gently into the trailer, he was focused on not being beaten.

We walked into the wide chute area toward the trailer, and I kept walking, again as if he and I had done this together a thousand times. I shared thoughts and pictures and sensations in my mind of a young, spirited bay horse traveling safely and comfortably to a place with a large grass pasture and the company of a young quarter horse mare. I saw the picture of him walking gently into the trailer, I felt, even before we stepped into the trailer, the rocking of the trailer floor, the sounds of hooves on the trailer floor, and the rattles you hear when it's holding the weight of a horse. All of these pictures and senses I shared with an open heart and offered to him in preparation of the next step in our journey. I felt how this particular trailer, on this particular day was destined to deliver a special horse to freedom.

Beyond any hope or expectation I could have had, he followed me straight into the trailer with no hesitation. No stopping to sniff, not even a blink of an eye, and he was standing in the trailer munching hay off the floor like an old pro.

He flicked his ears to let me know he understands, he's ready and it's time to go. So without ceremony, I closed the trailer door, climbed into the truck and headed home. At the time, I didn't even think to say goodbye to our audience, to talk to anyone or ask their response...all I remember was silence.

I called this giant horse in a small body Dufresne (pronounced doo-FRANE) after the main character in one of the most satisfying stories I know, "The Shawshank Redemption." Andy Dufresne, in the story, was wrongfully imprisoned for over twenty years, endured unspeakable abuse, and finally, quietly, revealed the injustices of his jailers and escaped through the sewer pipes to spend the rest of his days on a Pacific coast beach.

Dufresne settled into his new pasture home immediately. His wounds healed faster than wounds are supposed to heal, his hair grew back and he gained weight overnight.

He was immeasurably happy to give his attention, to learn about bathing, hoof care, and the other more pleasant parts of how humans and horses share their lives. Like a kid walking into a candy store for the first time, he'd walk around the pasture with long grass hanging out of his mouth, his whole body engaged in a smile, born again into a completely different world.

Whether we do use a round pen as a tool, if we use halters, whips, other equipment, the communication through our presence, our awareness of what we are bringing to the conversation is ultimately what the horses are listening to. They are always listening. Sometimes, we have a hard time hearing ourselves.

I don't know that Cooper was ever labeled a difficult or rank horse, that anyone ever "gave up" on him in one way or another. But I do know that his unique expression as a very intelligent, very connected horse was met with training techniques based in dominance. And this is what created his ability to "push people's buttons" on an energetic level, to know just how to stiffen up, when to explode, when to withdraw ... he feels it. It can be easy to take it personally because he's working on an emotional level. But all he's doing is telling us what he knows about how people work. This was his earliest training, and he was paying attention.

This is Dufresne in pasture the same day we picked him up.

Being A Human With A Horse

Sometimes I forget to use my own communication abilities. Sometimes I forget to create images, to adjust my presence, I forget to feel, and I get caught up in just getting something done. It's never a big tragedy -- Cooper lets me know immediately that my presence is occupied by my analytical thinking, that I have interrupted my connection. Usually, it looks like him thrusting his head down to the ground to nibble an almost non-existent tuft of something. I could punish him, I take it personally that the horse is trying to get the best of me and yank on his face with a rude energy. I could do those things. I could repeat an old pattern of an old presence of an old perspective and through repetition reinforce for him that people aren't listening. Sometimes it is tempting to go back into a fight!

To truly be in two-way communication with a horse means realizing that he is "training" me just as much as I am "training" him.

Horses, and all animals, communicate with images that are detailed with senses. As he plays his games, he is sharing images and senses. He is applying pressures that, when I give to him, he will cease to apply, thereby letting me know he got what he wanted. Sometimes he's communicating that he isn't getting what he wanted. This horse has command of human emotions, and he uses them to apply pressure when there is something he'd like different, or when he feels a challenge. When I am connected with him, I get to sense all of this as he shares it, and the more aware I am of myself, the easier it becomes for me to recognize what's really going on. When I have awareness, I am free to engage or not engage.

Without making it into a psychological study, without making it into a spiritual practice, horses are creatures with access to many different dimensions of awareness. The dimension they lack is the capacity to judge, or in other words, to use a mental capacity to create a sense of opposition or self-doubt within themselves.

In humanity, the vast majority of us have been taught, from a very early age, to doubt and question ourselves. In fact, it's one of the first things sold to us as very young people. We are taught to override what we know in our hearts. It can feel like an inner battle until maybe we numb ourselves to it, or just learn to ignore the tension in our body. The horses feel it, though.

"When do you suppose we will start taking Cooper and Dreamer out on trail rides together?" came Lynda's question.

"Well, he has invited the riding relationship," I begin to share, "so now it's just a matter of walking through that conversation with him. I'm not going to get on him unless we are on the same page about it."

There is a convention introduced by "natural horsemanship" that humans are predators and horses are prey animals, and this is how we should address them. It is a very interesting assumption that horses would see us in this way.

We can show up with a predatory energy, and the horses will respond from their instinctive flight response. This response is what a lot of trainers rely on. It is a power game where we hold all of the cards. Going back into the round pen, we then have a prey animal trapped in a cage and are doing what we can to manipulate its fear of being killed. Hopefully, it figures out that we mean no harm, and hopefully it figures out that anything we might ask should be received the same way. This is anxiety training, a form of one-way communication.

If we don't have a round pen, we can still use anxiety training with ropes, bits, spurs, whips and other equipment that will inflict pain and invoke the horse's instinctive prey response. Of course, these tools don't need to inflict pain, but when they do, they override any sense of equality between us and the horses. This has been effective for eons to train horses to submit to our will. I won't say it's all kindness, although these tools can certainly be used in kind ways. But humans have figured out that pain can be a great motivator and horses will, when pushed to a point of instinctive fear, give away their heart and their will to survive our demands.

Again, none of this is wrong. It has been effective for eons as horses have offered themselves freely to humanity for sport, companionship, service, battle, field-work, meat, milk and more.

People are, with exponential speed, realizing that there is a different way. We are noticing that dominance, while effective for some, does not create a truly partnering relationship. We are beginning to value relationships with animals. We are beginning to see that to be in relationship with an animal invites a different sort of awareness with ourselves, an awareness that has a magnificent ripple effect on the rest of our lives. The biggest obstacle for most people is the courage to see where we have been dominant, in fact predatory, and without punishing ourselves, simply choose another way.

In my conversation with Cooper, I have no expectation that he should carry me around the property, much less out in the forest, simply because he's "broke to ride." He's done it before, he's carried many riders, trainers, and he's even been out on this trail before. But there is no way I'm going to just hop up on his back and expect that he should do this for me, just because I'm a human in the saddle.

We have a conversation about the saddle. Maybe it lasts about ten minutes, but we consciously have the conversation. I bring into my presence that the saddle is part of our dance together, and I share with him my sense of how it can feel up on his back.

He responds with tension and a raised head, holding his breath, his muscles poised for defense. He is sharing his sense of how it feels to have the saddle on his back. I hear him.

He's had saddles thrown up on his back before and has had to stiffen up to endure it. No problem. I understand. I share with him that I get it. "Thank you for letting me know." And I stand with him, my presence demonstrating that I am a different perspective, giving him space to notice it. About six seconds later, he exhales, drops his head and works his mouth. I set the saddle gently on his back. "Thank you, my friend. I understand."

Within that six seconds, I felt sadness, anger, frustration, rage, fear, anxiety and exhaustion -- all sensations he has associated with the saddling process. I felt the sensations in my body, and because I am aware of my own presence, I know that these emotions are not about me. They are the old, stored up histories of his past. Listening, sensing these without taking them personally opens up new space for him to let them go, for us to move forward into a new conversation.

He turns to look at me. He's not tied. I don't want to trap him into this conversation. He's welcome to walk away. My presence is the same. If he walks away, it's not personal. It's not a statement about me. It's a statement of how he feels being saddled. And for me, it is an honor to receive his communication. I know we're still going forward into saddling, because he invited the riding relationship. To have a riding relationship, I require the use of a saddle … he's got some high withers!

This is all part of the communication through my presence. I have no apology for requiring a saddle. I have no anger for how others have saddled him in the past. I am the presence of a new perspective, a new conversation that invites us both into a riding relationship where neither of us finds a need to defend against each other. Neither of us is the predator, neither of us is the prey.

Have you ever noticed people trying really hard to buy into the predator/prey training techniques, and the horses just sit and stare at them? Have you wondered why this is? Or have you had thoughts like, "That person just needs to get more assertive! Just take a dominant stand!"

The horses know what is in our heart. They know when we are going against who we are, even when we are deceiving ourselves. Cooper is a horse who will let you know when you are not being who you are. His amazing mastery of emotional energy, of invasive energy, and his use of his body to bump, kick and throw - all of these are his communications that he senses incongruency.

I could try to fit him into a box labeled "This Is How All Horses Respond To Training," and get my butt thrown off. Or, I can listen to him, feel my own body, and step into a relationship of trust rather than dominance.

It can seem like developing this kind of relationship would take way longer than conventional training that uses force to make the horse perform. In truth, the road via listening can be far faster than the road via dominance. Two minutes of true, connected communication can do more than two weeks of repetition without awareness. And infinite patience brings immediate results. When we drop our need to have our expectations met, the horses can surprise us with how well they truly understand what we're asking for ... and we'll actually be available to see it!

The thing about being with horses, working and playing with horses, is that our well-developed attempts to train them are actually roads away from who we truly are. Following a training regimen takes our awareness away from our innate communication long enough to implement someone else's interpretation of what a horse "should" be. I'm not suggesting for a minute to throw away the wonderful tools shared with us by trainers from all of time and everywhere on the planet. I am, though, pointing your awareness back to the undeniable fact that no matter what system or teaching you use, it is still you standing right there with the horse. And you are not a system. Your horse does not see you as a system.

It comes time to share the girth with Cooper. Again, I have no opinion about the girth, I just know that it is a part of our riding relationship. I buckle one side so that it will be loose for him when I get over to the other side. As I pick up the girth, Cooper walks away, girth dangling.

I let him walk away.

I take notice of what's going on in my own body. There is a charge there, an emotion, right in my solar plexus. Could it be that I'm taking his behavior personally? Could it be that I think this has anything to do with me?

I take a breath and expand my presence again, remembering our conversation, remembering how it feels to be a different perspective. By this time, he has stopped over on the other side of the round pen, and he's watching me.

Through my presence, I let him know there is no punishment coming, that I am just walking over to buckle up the girth. His eyes relax, he works his mouth, and his head drops a bit. I step over to his left side, and this time, as I bring up the girth to buckle it, he stands beautifully still, breathing. I exhale, too.

These stories I'm sharing, the details of them, are permission. This is permission to be kind. So many horses have endured unkind cinching and have been expected to not speak about how it feels. Many are punished for speaking about how it feels. Of course, they will perform anyway. Of course, their answer will always be, "As you wish." But once we are aware of a different way, once we are capable of being a different perspective, this is permission to step into the kindness of it, fully.

As I have said before, going the route of kindness rather than dominance can seem like it will take eons longer to accomplish a task. And at first, that may seem true. It may actually take more time to invite a response that is given freely, especially when the invitation is truly to let go of strong resistance. Once the communication is clear, though, once the connection is acknowledged, there is no repetition necessary, and progress can happen in a way that defies convention.

It's been a couple of weeks now that I've been asking for Cooper's feet, to clean them, and because that's just something I really enjoy. I like cleaning feet! Satisfying! When we began, he offered to kick me with his right hind, and swung his hips into me when I asked for his left hind, finishing the dance by planting all of his weight on the foot I was asking for.

Now, many people would take this as something to be corrected, a "bad behavior." I can hear all of the voices of criticism ..."You can't let him do that!," "You have to make him give it to you," "He's not allowed to get away with that," "You need to be stronger with him, let him know that you are alpha," "He knows better than that -- next time he gives you his foot, hold onto it so he knows he can't just take it away from you," etc.

I just can't subscribe to those inflexible ways of thinking, not when it's so clear to me, through the tension in his body, because he's holding his breath, because he acts like he is incapable of standing on 3 feet, that the way he learned to play with people when asked for his feet is full of tension and battle. I have no interest in being in that conversation! And it's my sense that he doesn't, either.

A Little Bit Of Lightening

When I was introduced to Lightening, I was told that nobody could handle her or go near her without her biting or kicking them. There were stories of her pinning people in a corner and kicking them. She had a young foal at her side whose name was, of course, Thunder.

After one visit with her, it was clear that she was in pain and had probably been in pain for a long, long time. She had rope scars, crooked knees and battle wounds that told stories of some rough interactions with people.

She needed medical care, and I was told there was none available. She came with a reputation. I had to talk a vet into assisting me to tranquilize her, to care for her parallel front abscesses and provide us with some antibiotics. She and I did the rest on our own. Both feet were wrapped for at least a month. Having the pressure in her feet relieved took an edge off of her aggression, lucky for me, and I was able to groom her, do some healing work and begin to form a friendship.

About 3 months into it all (honestly, I'm not sure of the time frame – I wasn't paying attention to how long anything took; it was all about being with what showed up each day), her front feet were healed and her hooves growing. I was able to trim and care for all 4 feet, take her out for walks, wean her foal, etc.

One afternoon we were in the barn aisle and I was working on her left hind hoof. Her toe was resting on the ground, hip relaxed, and I was squatted down working with the hoof knife and rasp to clean up the rotten parts of her foot. As I remember it, out of nowhere she launched me across the barn aisle, just shoving me sideways with her hind leg. I knew it wasn't a response to physical pain. I knew it! And without knowing why it happened, my feelings were hurt. It felt like an automatic response in her, for something that had nothing to do with me. I know there was something in our interaction that opened the door to that response, but the fact that it happened, that she went there, just broke my heart after making myself so vulnerable to her since the day we met.

I started crying. Hard. Sitting on the step sobbing. And then I realized she was watching...

So I cried, and opened myself further, letting myself feel and show every little speck of frustration, sadness, hurt, anger, heartbreak, and everything else I was feeling. I hid nothing, and I remember talking to her with all of that emotion, saying, "Yeah ... this is how that feels! This is what it feels like to me that you just shoved me across the barn aisle!" And she watched me.

After a few minutes of raw truth together, she lowered her head, still watching me, and she opened up to communicate directly with me. I heard her realization distinctly, "People ... feel...?"

And I said, "YES! People DO feel."

My compassion soared as I realized what was actually going on here. First, the space that we shared, the openness we did have together invited her to express some of what was locked up inside of her – the shove she gave me was an expression of all of the frustration, sadness, anger, etc. she's been holding onto for who knows how long (mind you, that doesn't mean that the behavior is socially acceptable), but the clarity and understanding is what allows healing to happen. Second, when she shoved me, most of what I was feeling was the same as what she feels, and because we were both carrying those feelings, it was amplified between us, facilitating the awareness. Third, in her experience with people, there was never an interaction that let her integrate the reality that humans feel what's going on around them, within her or others – she got to see a different perspective. Fourth, I got to see a different perspective of myself, realizing that even when I think I'm being sensitive and "helping," it isn't always received that way. It wasn't humbling, it was an honor.

I stood up after a while and walked over to her. We were both exhausted. Her head hung low, vulnerable. I stroked her neck and shoulder, put my tools away, and brought her back to a clean, soft stall before I went into the house.

The next day, her behavior changed entirely – she was suddenly interested in what everyone in the barn was doing. She stopped trying to bite and we were now able to open her stall door with a stall guard so she could hang her head out and be with everyone; the kids could now lead her out for turnout time, groom her, pick her feet and love on her. We still needed to be aware of ourselves when we handled her, but the fear had dissolved. There was a whole new understanding, new awareness, not only in this one courageous horse, but in the people at the stable who watched the transformation. It's amazing what can happen when the heart expands.

A couple of weeks ago, I started asking for each of Cooper's feet, and as he would even shift his weight to offer one to me, I'd stop asking right there, stand up and love on him, "Thank you so much. Thank you," give him a rub, and ask again. This went well with all but the left hind, the one that he would plant with all of his weight, or, more often in the beginning, swing his hips into me, walking sideways toward me for about 12 feet.

Again, I could hear the criticisms in my mind, "You can't let him get away with that!", "You're teaching him bad habits!",

"He's going to think he can get away with that every time now!" But, those critical, fearful voices are not part of this conversation. Those voices are in a perspective of training a horse to respond to stimulus. My conversation with Cooper and his feet is not about training. It is about inviting him to share an understanding, a mutual space of no harm to each other. My presence and actions communicate that I intend no harm to him, and at the same time I communicate that I am not available to be harmed. In this kind of communication, results are not only imminent, but can become far more than we would have asked for.

It is not in a horse's nature to harm another without reason. Even as he swings his hips toward me, even as he lifts a hind leg as if he'll kick, he still intends no harm. He is simply communicating how he's feeling and showing his response to whatever stimulus he perceives at that moment. It's not personal to me. He's not out to get me. And listening from this perspective diffuses the anxiety, mine and his, almost instantly.

Letting It Be Beautiful

It had been over two weeks since I had cleaned his left hind foot. He just didn't want to give it to me freely. He would think about it, lift it up with great tension, and slam it back down again as if he was going to fall over right on top of me! And again, the voices of training say, "He's capable of standing on three legs, make him do it...he's 10 years old, he's done it a hundred times before...next time you get a hold of his foot, you just hold on and teach him he can't take it away..." No thank you. I'm not interested in a battle, and I'm not interested in being that person.

So what if his foot has dirt in it for two weeks? So what if it takes the time it takes? So what? The rewards of kindness outlast any criticism of how long it takes for a horse to respond willingly. Besides, all tolled up, the amount of time I spent asking for that left hind hoof over the past two weeks adds up to less than an hour, because that is what we were available for. Within that hour of time I shared kindness. I shared a different perspective.

I asked him today for his left hind foot, after we cleaned the other three. I asked and he shifted his weight off of it. "Thank you, Buddy." I asked again, and he gave me a surprise gift! He lifted his left hind foot and just held it in the air about 12 inches off the ground for me to clean! No slamming down, no avoidance, and he was breathing. I didn't grab it, but I did support it gently with one hand while I did a quick cleaning with the hoof pick. I finished fast and quit early while he was still holding his own foot in the air, and then I stood up...

"What a gift!" I celebrated! "Thank you so much, my friend! Wow...that was a real gift, thank you!" And I gave him hugs and rubs..."Holy smokes, wow, I wish everyone in the world could have seen this gift. You are so magnificent, thank you!" and more hugs...

The magic of all of this is the sincerity. He truly did give me a gift! You see, to me, this is not a horse with behavior problems, this is not a horse who bucked someone off, this is not a horse who will fight if given the chance, this is not a horse who is too smart for his own good...this is an amazing, beautiful being who happened to show up in a horse body. This is a unique intelligence and life who is so wired for connection that he is willing to play some very uncomfortable games with some unaware people in order to feel connection. This is my friend.

There are horses who respond to most people in mostly the same way. Call them stoic, call them dull, call them smart...they just are who they are no matter what person comes to them, asks of them, handles them.

Then, very much like sensitive people, there are horses whose mood and behavior will change very easily with the ambient energy. Even when things with one person are steady and wonderful, if another enters with a highly-charged emotional state, the sensitive horse will feel that energy and it can change their world view instantly.

Of course, every horse is an individual. Every horse responds a bit differently depending on who is with them, especially when there are vast differences in human emotional states. Can we honor their individualness in response to our own?

Cooper still holds a lot of anxiety in his body, in his way of being. He holds his breath when I ask to clean his hooves. He raises his head and his entire body becomes tense as I gently lay a light saddle pad on his back. He looks for escape, even when he is not physically restrained, at least in my perception, and communicates insecurity by grabbing with his mouth when I step back into his reach. As he and I dance together, he lets a lot of it go. He lets his breath out, works his mouth for 10-15 seconds straight, shakes his head side-to-side, all different ways of releasing stress from his neck. As this release is so new, he still has sort of an itchy trigger finger, you might say, to be reinfused with stress and begin with the games he knows how to play. He knows at least one way to be sure he's connected with someone, even if those games are uncomfortable.

If I had the expectation that we should be able to clean all of his feet in just the perfect way by now, I would be inviting a fight into my own world. He would feel that fight within me. I could go there.

But why would I when we have a conversation in kindness happening, and it just happens that working with the feet is the vehicle taking us on the ride?

Right or wrong, however it unfolds, horses are an opportunity to share a journey with another living being.

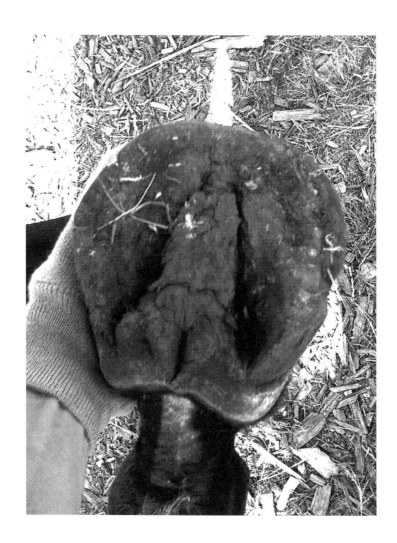

Unpredictability

Part of our time together each time we play is, when we are all finished dancing with the saddle, his halter comes off and he grazes anywhere he wants to be on the property. Well, the past couple of days, he thought it would be pretty cool to graze in the bird-seed bins on the back deck of the house! It's a good thing that deck is so well built!

First I heard the metal cans being bumped around. Then came the unmistakable sound of hooves on solid wood and thought, "Oh, man...here we go..." As I walked around the corner, sure enough, there he was, up on the back deck. There was someone in the house at that time, watching Cooper through the kitchen window - he came out and told Cooper, "Hey! NO!" and instantly the ambient energy shifted to high anxiety.

Cooper, already prepared for tension, responded reflexively to the anxiety by looking for escape. By that time, I had arrived with a halter in hand, and our human friend had gone back into the house. But Cooper had already switched into stress-escape mode.

He didn't give us big ugly escape behavior, but he thought about it. He tested it with his presence as I touched his body. The moment my hand touched his shoulder, his neck and shoulder went stiff like they do when he wants to invade and defend. Only this time, it wasn't invasion he was exploring. In a matter of 1.6 seconds, he ran through a series of "questions": "is she going to chase me?", "is she going to yell and swing things?", "do I run?", "what do I need to defend against?." And I felt him tuck himself away behind the very familiar facade of a tough, defended horse who knows he can us physical size and power to escape or invade at any time.

So be it, I felt. If he's going to run away, I can't stop him physically. But even giving over to "what will be will be," I was still going to show up as a different perspective. I felt the anxiety of our human friend in the house. I felt the anxiety of the horse in front of me. My own mind can produce all of the scenarios for what could go wrong...but why would I go there? Why would I give myself over to that vibration of ambient anxiety, even if it was now quite potent?

By this time, Cooper found a new way to entertain himself. He had a seed sock full of thistle meant for goldfinches in his mouth, dismantling the apparatus it hung from. Yes, he is creative! I brought the halter up to him, offering to guide him off of the deck. His first response was a threat to run away. Hmmm. Yes, that makes sense, but it's not the conversation I'm here to have. And I exhaled to shift the space.

The exhale and my awareness that I wouldn't be overcome by anxiety invited him to slow down just a little bit and wait for the halter. I did have to wrestle the bird sock out of his mouth, though...sigh. So, we saved the seed sock, put on the halter and started walking off the deck. It's actually a pretty magnificent sound, hooves on solid wood. Enjoying the sensation of the sound begins to diffuse the anxiety.

The anxiety was still pushing up into the red zone, though. On our walk back to the paddock, he offered to bolt a couple of times, to charge past me, which is one of his well-practiced tricks. It is preceded by a wave of stress that blows straight through my body and makes him feel like a brick wall walking behind me. It makes me feel like I'm made of paper.

I feel it, I honor what he's sharing with me, because what I'm sensing is his communication of how he's feeling. It could be interpreted as a personal threat, but that would be a misinterpretation.

I am not available to be hurt, or trampled. My presence communicates this gently, congruently, and I exhale again, turning slightly toward him, eyes up, with the suggestion that he just not do it.

The bottom line is, he knows he's stronger than me, he knows he can escape at any time. He's done it many times before with several people, and with me. It isn't my dominance that invites his response to abandon the plan to charge away, it is my presence that is unavailable to that behavior. It is the suggestion that our connection remains intact as he stays with me. In this instance, my presence became the more potent ambient energy as he and I walked together. The anxiety was still there, and I would never deny it. But I do have the ability to amplify my own presence beyond the anxiety and create a potent suggestion that overrides the "anxiety auto-pilot."

His response was delightful, actually. Considering he was ready to prove a point and just blast off, his response and shift to just walk with me, to join me in what I was available for was quite a gift. After the gift earlier in the afternoon of offering his hind foot without resistance, I'd say it was a magnificent day.

Appreciating Humanity

People are only capable of seeing in another as much as they are available to see within themselves. And even when they are available to see more, they may choose not to by some very potent means. It's not a linear statement, it is dimensional. We don't have to be consciously aware of what we're available to in ourselves, but we will find out when we're given the opportunity to see, or dominate, the life and beauty in another, no matter their species or form of life.

Many people see horses as animals requiring training. They'll see a problem waiting to happen. They'll see a big feed bill or piles of manure.

Others will see a being of light presenting as a horse. They may see a shamanic totem animal, a power animal, and feel reverence from afar.

What we see in horses is as diverse as who we are, each of the 7+ billion of us here on the planet at this time.

There has been the movement that horses are pristine mirrors for us, which is perfect when we need them and their expression to be about Us. When we remember who we are, though, when we remember the purity and truth of our own existence, then we can step away from taking even the horses' "positive" messages personally. The horses will always show up and let everything we do be about us. Their message is perpetually, "As you wish." And when the day comes when we can ask, "Will you show me more about you?" we step into a whole new level of communion. This is accessible to us at any time. It is our birthright to be in this kind of communion.

Our ability to hear them is limited only by our expectation that communication must happen in a certain way. Ultimately, the more we understand about the communication we bring to the conversation, the more available we become to see who a horse truly is. At that point, it's not about Us.

But that's the $7 billion question, isn't it? Who am I, really?

And here's another good one..."How do I know if I'm right?"

If I tried to be "right" in what I'm doing with Cooper, how much would that invite him to challenge me? How much would that be me bringing the battle to him? And how much space is in there to doubt myself?

When I doubt myself, how much am I actually looking to Cooper to make up for where I'm just not certain, hoping he'll understand even though I'm not even sure I know what I'm asking?

It's so common. It's all based in fear. And it's okay.

Now, we can say that fear is "bad", but what does that accomplish? Then we're in a fight with fear, which, shockingly, keeps the fear alive! By and large, we have been taught to doubt ourselves from a very early age, to question our choices, to run our thoughts through a system of filters and sieves designed to compare our thoughts to everyone else's, to evaluate whether our choices are "good", to create places to hide and retreat to in case someone else can point to us and say, "that's bad."

The horses don't live there. They will believe us, no matter if what we're saying comes from our heart or through the filters of judgment. They expect no apology from us because they have no judgment of us. Their love is not about earning; they are in love, with us, no strings attached.

Somewhere along the lines, humans have been taught that it is scary to know their own hearts. The horses show up ready to receive our hearts in every moment, with no judgment or evaluation of what's there.

Judgment can sound like, "He should know that I don't need him to bark incessantly. Tell him it's a waste of all of our energy." Or, "My horse has been down that trail a hundred times - there is no reason for her to have anxiety." These opinions are totally valid, and there is nothing wrong with them. But going forward in this frame of mind will lead to a journey of battles, trying to prove our rightness to the horse or ourselves, rather than inviting a connection. It will lead to finding problems to fix rather than creating effective, kind interactions.

And the amazing beauty of it all is, the animals will say to us, without fail, no matter if we are judging or open to clarity, "As you wish."

We've been taught that it is safer to satisfy others than to speak our truth and walk our unique walk. But is that really safety? The horses feel much safer with us when we are honest with ourselves.

There are times with Cooper, and with other horses, when I feel I slip into a void. I feel like I don't know what I'm doing, like I don't know what's next. I feel like the horse disconnects from me. I feel alone, and it feels emotional. In those times, it can feel very compelling to go into dominance mode - I do know very well how to fill the void with pressure tactics to bend a horse's behavior to my will. That open space of a void, though, can be filled with other things, too.

The only time the dominance route can overcome me is when I make the horse's behavior seem to mean something about me, as if his resistance or disconnection is a statement that there is something wrong with me, or what I have done. Dominance only takes control when I take his behavior personally.

Several times in the round pen Cooper breaks energy with me and walks off to nibble grasses on the other side of the fence. What a grand invitation to me to get very clear on what I'm bringing to the conversation!

Generally, I just go sit on the mounting block and enjoy the sunshine. I give him all the space in the world to be proving a point, if that's what it is, or to take a break, if that's what it is, or to go into avoidance, if that's what it is...but I don't go searching for why he's doing what he's doing. I just let him do it. His body is safe, my body is safe, and my presence, my perspective is about inviting a conversation of communion, true two-way communication. Not dominance.

I certainly could get the lunge whip and make him work in the round pen until he realizes that when he walks away from me he has to work harder and when he stands next to me he doesn't. I could do that. But that's feels quite a lot like hazing, making someone work really hard to earn a false friendship. No thanks on that one.

There is a time and a place where I would send a horse away from me, I suppose, if I felt in imminent danger or something close to that. But I'd rather walk away myself than create such punishment.

So, he steps away, I go sit down and enjoy myself in the sunshine. And wouldn't you know it, about 30 seconds later, there he is again, coming over to say hello! I greet him with love, the kind of love like he's been gone forever, the kind of love we love to get from our dog when we get home at the end of the day. Why should it matter that someone else thinks he should know this or that by now? What if each and every time we are with our horse we express our heart and appreciation as if it's the first time we've seen them in months, or years, or ever?

Anima-Morphize

To anthropomorphize is to attribute human form or personality to things not human. Today I looked at the reverse of that. I looked at what it is to assign animal form or personality to humans, and I came up with a new word.

Animamorphize: to attribute animal characteristics and/or behaviors to things not of the animal kingdom

Science tried to convince us a while ago that our species can be categorized as part of the animal kingdom. If we are speaking of just the physical existence of humans, just the body, that could almost make sense. Bless the heart of science for trying! But so much of being a human is about our awareness and the creative functionality of our own consciousness, a trait which is uniquely different than the animal kingdom.

To explore further what I already knew in my heart, I started looking at the concept of dominance. We watch the animal kingdom communicate with one another through physical behaviors and other silent, not silent, and energetic "languages". We have observed, studied, measured and recorded how they build their social structures and determine who plays which role in the community (herd, pack, gaggle, etc). We have labeled their behaviors as aggression, dominance, submission, feeding, reproduction, seeking shelter, etc., and once those labels were in place, by and large, there didn't seem to be much reason to expand our understanding of what we saw. Everything seemed to fit into one of our categories.

In humanity's search to know itself, we've sought to apply survival terms to ourselves as well. It's a bit of a chicken and egg discussion – did we see survival behavior and emulate it, or did we observe our own behavior and categorize it?

We watch certain animals create stress, pain and sometimes injury. We call it dominant behavior. We watch animals give up their space, become smaller, move out of the way. We label that behavior subordinate. We watch the animals whose behavior we have labeled dominant take control of the movement and resources of other animals. We saw how effective "dominance" is in survival, because it would lead to more survival in a very linear, 1:1 fashion.

Aggression expressed as dominance leads to survival among animals. Human interactions and systems use the same terminology. Systems like business and government and religion. Even in cultures and families we use dominance to control the survival and behaviors of ourselves and one another. Survival of the fittest, the strong survive – applied within humanity, these concepts use battle and competition to create a very strained and controlled survival.

Power, dominance and control have been used as the most immediately effective ways to survive and lead. Perhaps the consciousness of humanity was not yet available to create another way. Or perhaps humanity decided the fastest and most powerful approach to survival, to simply dominate others, was of the greatest value. In so doing, we perpetuated the perspective that it is "good" to be the dominant force.

Now, though, a much greater number of us are available to a different perspective. Leading through dominance will always be an effective way to create power and control. But much of humanity is becoming disinterested in recognizing leadership expressed as power and control. We are seeing the ripple effect and exponential benefit of leading by example and empowering each other's unique gifts, awareness and abilities. Through this empowerment we're starting to see new types of creations for coexistence in our lives. New systems and new perspectives.

Survival no longer requires the destruction of individuals or life forms to understand or expand humanity's innate strength and presence on the planet. In other words, we don't need to weed out the weak in order to force new innovation and evolution. We are beginning to recognize innate value in the creativity and expression of all entities, whether they are small, medium or large.

Describing humanity as a member of the animal kingdom served to open our awareness and compassion to the other species who share our planet. But as a species, we are not of the animal kingdom, as our consciousness is vastly different. To continue our systems of dominance, power and control for the ultimate goal of survival at this point will actually create the opposite effect.

It is time to recognize and honor human consciousness as designed to create rather than survive. The animal kingdom will also evolve in consciousness in response to humanity creating new forms of coexistence. We don't need to be like the animal kingdom and they don't need to be like us. Within this realization is a foundation for new and brilliant coexistence between all species. Anthropomorphizing and animamorphizing can then contribute as simple and profound tools for compassion, clarity and understanding rather than systems and models to live by, or against.

Animals learn life and survival by default, through observation, trial and error and a sense of reason that is absent of the judgments that dictate a majority of human decisions. We, with a different consciousness, have the capacity to facilitate each others' awareness and empower the freedom of perspective and compassion as tools of creation.

The power of dominance has a relatively short shelf life. The expansive effects of empowering and facilitating each others' brilliance, however, we have only begun to explore.

What Are We Really Talking About Here?

What is so scary about love?

When Cooper walks away from me, does he still love me?
When he walks toward me, does that mean he loves me?
When he gives me what I ask for, does that mean he loves me?
When he eats the food I give him, does that mean he loves me?
When he bucks me off, does that mean he doesn't love me?
When he uses his invasive energy tactics, does he not love me?
What does it all MEAN???? And how do I KNOW???

What if it means nothing? What if it's just behaviors?

Love is a vibration that is absent of judgment. It is a vibration
we know innately, intuitively, knowingly. Even those of us
who would deny the suggestion that they know love do know
love on a vibrational level.

Horses, and the animal kingdom, embody love. They embody
truth. They are incapable of denying themselves of who they
truly are. This is the great difference between humanity and the
rest of the kingdoms that share our planet. We are the only ones
with the capability of deceiving ourselves about who we truly
are. But we can't deceive the animals.

They are just as in love and enamored with us as we are with them. They are the space that is absent of judgment. And, they are available to respond to us, as the unique individuals that they each are. We can call it their personality, or use other creative terms that honor uniqueness. And though one horse may have a stoic personality, and another may have an energetic personality, is one more capable of love than another? Can we segregate them by how much love they have to share?

Certain uniqueness in personalities of animals can activate and speak to certain personalities of people. But it doesn't mean that one animal loves one type of person more than another. We may see a difference in response, in behavior. But that's just behavior. It's not love. The love is much bigger. It is constant. Perpetual. Unconditional.

We can categorize behaviors and make them mean something about us, but why would we want to work that hard? Why would we do that to ourselves? Truly...why would we do that to ourselves? What behaviors do we need to see to be convinced that we are loved?

We've been conditioned for so long to evaluate our own behaviors, to make behaviors mean something about our value, our worth, what we've earned, whether we make others comfortable or uncomfortable, and how that affects our survival, our success. And it can be very easy to assign that same system of judgments to the animals. It just makes sense that we would - it has been our survival mechanism for eons. Many will stick with it, finding the comfort of the familiar to be more valuable than the discomfort of the unfamiliar, even when the familiar isn't really working for us anymore. There is endless love for those who stay within their comfort zones.

Many others step into a different way of being, finding the discomfort of a new way of being to be more welcoming than the confines of what it takes to survive in the world of filters and judgments. And there is endless love for those who step into a different way.

The horses are in love at all times, and by that, what I am really saying is, they are always in a state of unconditionality, without judgment, without evaluation. Their relationship with survival has nothing to do with surviving their own doubt - they do not undermine or deceive themselves of their own unique truth. They just want their body intact with the opportunity to shake off the stress when it's all over. It is never a statement about you, your value or your "rightness", unless you want to make it so.

In every interaction, the animals are listening to us without an expectation of who we are "supposed" to be – they will respond to us no matter how we show up and communicate, "Okay, this is how it feels to be me in this environment." The more we let go of the expectation of who our animals are supposed to be, and the expectation of who WE are supposed to be, the more we become available to see who is standing right in front of us, no matter what species they are.

Getting It Right

The relationship I have with Cooper is different than the relationship between Lynda and Cooper. Their journey to ride together out on the trail will unfold at its own pace. Their sense of safety with each other will evolve. Every partnership with a horse, an animal, another person, is its own unique journey.

What I do know is that there is new space in Cooper's world for people of a different perspective. He has now expanded his world-view to include something other than dominance. The reason I know it is because I watched it happen. I felt it happen. That he shifted in my own presence, and I felt that shift in my own body as well, is the communication that more is now possible in his world. What an honor it is to be a part of that, even for one moment.

Other people who spend time with Cooper, who share their lives with him in any way have the opportunity to dominate and control him or to listen to him, as they wish. The only way they can get it right is if they judge that there is a right way to be. The horses will still show up to give to them, whether they are getting it right or wrong.

Your Ability To Expand Into A Bigger Perspective

Cooper is a horse. He will think, respond and express himself as a horse.

Humans are humans. They will think, respond and express themselves as humans. Even when humans observe, study and emulate horses and think we've got it down, we will still be humans.

Even humans who operate differently than the majority, those who have been considered to be disabled, strange, behind, or way too far ahead, are still expressing themselves simply as who they are.

The animal kingdom demonstrates sensory communication, and we have the ability to activate and use our own. Autism and other ways of being that were called disabilities simply because they were misunderstood are also invitations to expand into more of who we are. We can take the opportunity or walk away.

When the priority changes from trying to train, fix or alter anyone or anything outside of ourselves, and becomes all about knowing and embodying what it is we'd like to communicate, the entire world changes to accommodate and facilitate.

As humanity evolves, as awareness expands and the vibration continues to arise, the innate and subtle forms of communication will play a bigger and bigger part in how we interact with each other. The sensory communication, and our awareness of it, will be vital to understanding each other and creating life together. The days of judging how we say what we say, judging whether we should be different than we are, dissolve into interactions with the courage to see the communication that is actually happening, outside of offensive or defensive agendas.

Listening like a horse is listening without judgment. It is sensing what is actually happening and showing up and telling the truth from our heart. Horses don't need people to be different than they are. Horses don't need anything to be different than it is. But, they will make changes in their own world through communication and relocation, when possible, in response to their sense of their own highest good.

We can pass judgment if we'd like, to say that horses are selfish for following their own senses without compromise. Or we can listen.